GW00362514

Interrogating Irish Policies

William Kingston

School of Business, Trinity College, Dublin

Dublin University Press

© William Kingston
2007

All rights reserved. No part of this publication may be reproduced, stored in a retrieval system or transmitted in any form or by any means, electronic, mechanical or photocopying, recording, or otherwise without the prior permission of the publisher.

Published by
Dublin University Press,
Unit B2,
Bluebell Industrial Estate,
Dublin 12.
Tel: +353 1 456 9555
Fax: +353 1 4569599
Email: dup@brunswickpress.ie

Interrogating Irish Policies

Contents

Preface

A time when the country continues to enjoy unprecedented growth in wealth may not seem to be the best one to re-publish a series of articles which question public policies. However, little of this wealth can be attributed to policies other than those of getting as much money as possible from the EU and offering low taxation to inward foreign investors. There is the beginning of awareness in the country that both of these are losing effectiveness, with which is associated the feeling that the good times are not going to last. Consequently, another argument for casting a cold eye on earlier policies is that the day is approaching when better ones will be needed.

All the pieces which follow, except for the final one, which has been specially written for this collection, were originally published in Journals or as Chapters in books. This inevitably means that some of their contemporary references have been overtaken by events, but because the broad thrust of Irish policy has remained consistent throughout the period of their publication, this equally broad thrust of criticism of it has not dated. There is inevitably some repetition in the articles, since they were written for different readerships, but nothing has been done about this either, on the ground that what is repeated is generally the most important point that was sought to be made.

The best approach to the collection, therefore, might be to follow Chapter I with Chapter XI, and then to seek out the supporting information and arguments which are sandwiched between them.

The Chapters fall into four broad sections. The first of these is generally described by the title of the first Chapter, 'Belief in the superior wisdom of the State...,' followed by 'The Lemmings of Democracy,' which first explained why this belief is exceptionally strong in Ireland. The harm of 'clientelism' is now much more widely recognised than it was when this article originally appeared. It was argued in it that 'the question of whether democracy can survive or not comes down to whether or not there is some externally imposed constraint on the market for votes which fulfils a corresponding function to the constraints which are automatic in other markets.' In the Irish case, the EU, with all its faults, has provided such a constraint for nearly two thirds of all legislation. Although less evident, the value of this may be much more than its financial transfers.

In the next section, 'Why Ireland failed to keep up,' 'Entrepreneurship or

Rent-seeking?' and 'New Property Rights are Better than State Involvement,' discuss the consequences of this credulity about what the State can do in the Irish context.

The bureaucracy plays a particularly important role in a State built on such a belief, so a third group of articles includes 'What Can We Do About the Civil Service?' '"Systemic Corporate Failure of Public Administration:" Reflections on the Travers Report,' and 'An Alternative Agenda for Public Service Reform.'

The fourth group contains two articles which make practical proposals. These are 'A Patent System To Suit Ireland?' and 'The Financing of New Businesses.' If Irish belief in the superior wisdom of the State were ever to be replaced by belief in individual creativity acting within humane laws of property, these indicate some lines along which such laws would have to be developed. The final Chapter, 'Nice Rents If You Can Get Them,' revisits the themes of the earlier articles and adds some new ideas to them.

I thank the TCD Association and Trust and the School of Business in Trinity College, Dublin, for financially supporting this publication, and I also also owe much to my colleagues in that School and throughout the University for their many intangible contributions to it. But I am particularly grateful to my colleague, Dr. Kevin Scally of University College, Cork, without whose painstaking and generous editorial work this collection would never have been put together.

WILLIAM KINGSTON,
School of Business,
Trinity College Dublin.
e-mail: wkngston@tcd.ie

Chapter I

'Belief in the superior wisdom of the State...'

(First published 2006)

Introduction

A State has only two broad options about how to run its economy: it can develop laws, especially laws of property, which result in markets within which individuals are free to follow their own interests; or it can actively intervene. Apart from other pressures on modern politicians and public servants, they are invariably seduced by the belief that they can do better than the market. Every such intervention lessens competition and results in rent (which is the measure of the absence of competition). The term 'rent-seeking' then covers both the activity of capturing rents and that of getting the government to intervene so as to generate them.

Historically, the combination of law and property rights has always worked better, and indeed the wealth of the western world has depended heavily on it: in the words of the great economic historian, David Landes, 'those economies grew fastest that were freest' (1970, 19). Furthermore, because genuinely free markets maximize opportunities, they work against inequality in wealth and high prices. But the last thing business men want is a free market, so they will invariably do all they can to have the laws bent to suit themselves. They now find this easy enough, because the interests of politicians and bureaucrats are best served, not by the exacting task of trying to make humane property laws, but by intervening in the economy. And unfortunately, as Keynes's biographer, Robert Skidelsky, put it, 'this belief in the superior wisdom of the state breeds pathologies which deform, and at the limit destroy, the political economies based on it' (1995, xiii). The basic principle is that if we do not get the laws right, intervention will not work, and to the extent that we can get them right, it is unnecessary.

The limiting case of intervention is despotism, whose power to destroy economies has been demonstrated many times after the withdrawal of the great powers from their colonies during the twentieth century. Some members of the Business Studies Department, incidentally, gained first-hand experience of this through the external diploma in Management which Trinity granted in the Sudan during the 1980s, where they encountered some of Skidelsky's 'pathologies' operating close to their limit.

Rent-seeking in the Irish Free State

The Irish Free State came into being through such a colonial withdrawal, but although the potential for a market economy in the newly independent country was damaged, it was not destroyed. One reason why a property rights structure remained intact here was the combination of the influence of the Catholic Church with the great amount of property it owned. Both the first Constitution and the 1937 one had strong clauses protecting particular kinds of property rights because of this. An unanticipated and unfortunately malign consequence has been that this protection is invariably invoked to stymie any proposal to tax increased land values properly.

The second reason why these kinds of property in Ireland were untouched, ironically, was the way de Valera thought about them. He was not interested in economic development, but in ending Partition. Private non-Church property in the Free State (other than land subject to annuities under earlier British legislation) was mainly held by Protestants, and de Valera wanted to be able to show Northern Unionists that Protestants in the South did not suffer from native rule. His remarkable generosity to Trinity College, still a symbol of the Union, whose Officer Training Corps actually had a fatal casualty in fighting the 1916 rising, is only one example of this.

Serious rent-seeking in the Free State began in the time of the very first (Cumann na nGael) government, which gave Carroll's (the 'Catholic' tobacco firm) preferential excise duty. Gallaher's of Belfast regarded this as such blatant discrimination that they abandoned the Free State market completely, and did not return to it until after World War II. The same government's Shannon Scheme was also a State operation which pre-empted a private enterprise proposal to develop the hydro-power of the Liffey (Manning and McDowell 1984, 13-14, 28). One of the most striking examples of successful rent-seeking in that period, or indeed even later, was the Irish Hospital Sweepstakes. The specific legislation for this made it possible for a former Government Minister and his associates to become very rich indeed, as they were entitled to more than twice the proportion of today's National Lottery for expenses (Acts of the Oireachteas 1930).

Lemass's policies

The first government had also established Irish Sugar, but when Fianna Fail came to power in 1932 intervention in the economy through similar State-owned bodies and protected industries, accelerated dramatically. De Valera could never have liked Lemass's policies, but had to put up with them, because in setting up the protected industries, Lemass was providing a significant and continuing source of revenue for the Fianna Fail party, as payoffs for the rents arising from their quotas and tariffs (Daly 1992, 110, 179; cf. McCague 1994, passim).

Both approaches failed, precisely through lack of the discipline which economic competition within a legal framework imposes on participants. It is actually possible to track the dates of establishment of State-owned bodies according to the degree of relaxation of desirable requirements such as sinking funds for their capital. Nor did the appointment of inexperienced party supporters to their Boards help them to be managed well.

Lemass's Control of Manufactures Acts reflected the only economic philosophy which the new State had, that of Freidrich List's argument for protection of infant industries. This had been a leitmotiv of Arthur Griffith's economic writings in his journal, Sinn Fein, before independence. List's case had been very acceptable to the authorities in Germany as they tried to deal with Britain's head start in the industrial revolution. Also, the United States has been so successful at presenting itself to the world as the home of free enterprise that it is generally overlooked that it has always been strongly protectionist, right from Alexander Hamilton's publication of his Report on Manufactures in 1791 (which was an inspiration for List).

Protection undoubtedly worked in Germany and America, so why not in Ireland? One part of the answer is clear from nothing more complex than Adam Smith's insistence on the importance of 'the size of the market.' In both those countries, the market could support many firms, which meant that there was competitive advantage to firms which innovated – Andrew Carnegie's in steel in the U.S., and that of the Siemens brothers in electricity in Germany being classic examples. In Ireland, when the policy of protecting industry was introduced, if the small market could justify local manufacture at all, it could only be by a single firm. Lemass was quite clear-sighted about this: He told the Directors of Dunlop, for example, that unless they set up a tyre manufacturing plant in Cork, he would grant the monopoly of the Irish market to a competitor.

In many industries, advantage was taken of the Control of Manufactures Acts by British firms which simply transferred their obsolete plant and designs to Irish subsidiaries. The requirement of majority local ownership of the manufacturing plants was rendered ineffective by the device of setting up a sales company (which was not restricted in this way) as well. This made the monopoly profits, as the sole buyer at close to cost price, from the manufacturing firm which had the Irish shareholders. Clearly, the last thing to be expected from such firms was innovation, nor was there any. Most of the infant industries were destined to remain infants for ever, so that in the end, Lemass had no option but to turn his back on his own creation and see them off.

The move to an open economy

Just as the policies of intervention with which Sean Lemass is associated had actually been started by an earlier government, so the intellectual basis for the later change linked to his name, to an open economy, had actually been laid during the two Inter-party governments. T. K. Whittaker had learned his economics by doing an external London University degree, and his ideas for radical change owed much to this. It was the Fine Gael Minister of Finance at the time, Gerard Sweetman, who promoted him in the civil service into a position where he could work to put them into practice. He was also allowed to express them in a paper for the Statistical and Social Enquiry Society to gauge public reaction, and only when the sky didn't fall as a result, was the famous 'Grey Book' published. A second theoretical factor was that in those years the Central Statistics Office was able to make use for the first time of the techniques of national income estimation which had been developed in the U.S., mainly by Simon Kuznets. These measures showed that Ireland was actually in economic decline at the time.

But in spite of Keynes's claim in his great peroration to the General Theory that 'soon or late, it is ideas, not vested interests, that are dangerous for good or evil' (1936, 384) radical change needs something more than an intellectual basis. The practical factor which was decisive for acceptance of Whittaker's arguments, had also come into play before Lemass returned to power. This was the attraction of inward foreign investment, and this did not begin as an instrument of deliberate policy, but to a significant extent by accident.

The first inter-Party government had set up the Industrial Development Authority, and done the groundwork for financial incentives to get industry to the other side of the Shannon, because so many of the Control of Manufactures Acts firms had been located within the Pale. An Austrian firm, Liebherr, had pioneered tower cranes for building, and wanted to get into the British market, but the 1950s were not propitious years for a firm from a recently enemy country to set up manufacture in the U.K. They discovered that if they came to Ireland, in particular to Killarney, where the physical environment reminded them of home, they could have free access to the British market, and substantial capital grants as well.

Liebherr was followed by many other German firms, and it was this which laid the foundation for the regime which was available later on when U.S. firms, faced with the protective measures of the European Common Market, had no option but to establish manufacturing facilities inside its boundaries. By far the most important element of this country's ability to attract foreign investment has been its low business taxation regime – in fact, near-zero taxation for many years, until the EU insisted on a change. But it was Liebherr, not politicians nor civil servants, that paved the way for this. As Dr. Beddy, the Government's overseer of all industrial development at the time, told me, 'It would never have occurred to us that the West of Ireland incentives could bring in industry from abroad.'

When Lemass came back to the Department of Industry and Commerce, therefore, both elements for change, a developed theory and some practical examples, were waiting for him, and he pursued the new objectives with the same energy as he had applied to the former infant industry regime.

Proportional representation

A factor which has contributed greatly to making rent-seeking characteristic of the Irish economy is the proportional representation electoral system, which was imposed on both parts of the country by Britain as a device for preventing oppression of minorities. It was quickly abandoned in the North, but became so embedded in the South as even to be able to withstand attempts by de Valera to change it by referendum. The extent to which democracy can work depends upon a balance between property rights that are independent of the State on the one hand and the power of numbers on the other (see Usher, 1981). Multi-seat P.R. gives more power to numbers than the straight vote or list systems, and this consequently makes the electoral cycle correspondingly more dominant in all governmental decisions here. Because P.R. makes it so difficult for any party to obtain an overall majority, Irish Governments have always been vulnerable to rent-seeking by small groups which control a mere few seats.

Another aspect of how the centre cannot hold in Irish democracy is the weakness of the essential discipline of Cabinet collective responsibility, which is often flouted by individual Ministers for the sake of personal electoral advantage. Donough O'Malley notoriously announced free education for all without telling the Cabinet. More recently, the Ministerial announcement that all over-70s were to be given medical cards was made before there was any serious costing of the proposal. Since the promise simply could not be kept without the doctors' cooperation, their Union was consequently in a superb rent-seeking position in fixing the price for it. The result is that what the State now has to pay G.P.s for having an over-70 individual (who may be rich) on their list is a multiple of that for a younger person who will certainly be poor. Professional groupings, as well as public sector trades unions, have shown themselves to be particularly effective rent-seekers. The observation that a national budget 'can be regarded as a gigantic rent up for grabs for those who can exercise the most political muscle' (Muller 1989, 243) has been well demonstrated in many Irish instances.

A vivid illustration of the effect of the P.R. electoral system, combined with rent-seeking by civil servants, emerged from research by an American student on the Trinity MBA Course. She wanted to compare protection of infant industries in the Irish and U.S. contexts and was advised to try to interview Sean Lemass, then retired. She charmed much fascinating information out of him, including that when he came into the Department of Industry and Commerce in 1932, two Principal Officers had a proposal for a nitrogenous fertiliser industry. There was absolutely no economic justification for this, but they brought it back to him again and again, until in exasperation he told them, 'Look, I never want to hear anything more about this, but if you can ever persuade the Department of Finance to endorse it, I promise that I will make one of you Chairman and the other Managing Director' (Synon 1970).

They did eventually get these jobs, but not because the Department of Finance gave way. What happened was that Fianna Fail lost a seat in Wicklow, so that for electoral purposes the factory (which would have been uneconomic anywhere) was set up in Arklow, possibly the worst possible site for it in the whole country. Its little harbour has only nine feet of water on the bar, which cut out any economic importation of raw material by sea, and apart from all other diseconomies and the environmental damage it caused, as long as the plant existed, special trains carrying ammonia had to run daily between it and Cork.

Intellectual property

Because of the scale of their market, the Germans had been able to reconcile protection with innovation. They were also the first to discover just how useful intellectual property could be in providing a legal framework for the risky business of financing investment in research and development. Amongst other advantages, it made them so dominant in the pharmaceutical industries that it was only when German patents in Britain and the United States were sequestrated during World War I that important indigenous industries of this kind were able to develop in those countries (see Liebenau 1988).

The British, in contrast, were much less aware of the value of intellectual property - it took them until 1904 to give themselves as good a patent law as the Germans had had since 1877, for example. This disinterest was passed on to the new Irish State, whose whole legal structure was composed of the same statutes (until comparatively recently, it could truly be said that 'the Irish law on anything is the last British Act but one'). Also, at the very top of the British civil service, there was determination to give whatever guidance could help the new State to success. (An aspect of this which Mr. de Valera would hardly have liked to be generally known at the time, was that right up to the outbreak of war in 1939, there was an open telephone line between the Treasury in London and Merrion St. (O'Halpin 1989). Since both in terms of law and of attitudes, intellectual property was so unimportant in Britain, it would have been surprising if its potential had been grasped in Ireland. There was almost no chance that it could have been viewed positively, through German eyes, as it were.

Joining the Paris Convention

This is illustrated by how the country sleepwalked into membership of the body which administers patents and trademarks internationally. The Paris Convention for the Protection of Industrial Property dates from 1883, and its member countries meet at roughly 10-year intervals to agree on procedural matters. One of these gatherings was scheduled for the Hague in 1925, and the year before, the Irish Governor-General received a letter from the Foreign Office in London, 'assuming that they would represent the Irish Free State at this meeting.' Foreign relations had indeed been reserved to the Imperial Government in the Home Rule Bill, which had been passed in August 1914 but then suspended for the duration of the war. However, nobody seems to have told the Foreign Office people that the country had become independent in the interim by a different means, so that they were no longer needed.

Since we were certainly not going to allow the British to represent us, we would have to go ourselves, but the question of a Ministerial delegation to the Hague meeting was never discussed. On a day when Patrick McGilligan, the responsible Minister (of Industry and Commerce) was out ill, as he often was, two of his civil servants went to Mr. Cosgrave as President of the Executive Council, and sold him the idea that they should go to the Hague Conference on their own. There, with the assistance of Count O'Kelly de Gallagh, one of the very few foreign representatives the Free State had at the time, they signed the country into the Paris Convention. Two years later, McGilligan introduced a patents bill in the Senate, saying that 'the best thing for us to do is whatever the Convention requires,' in apparent total lack of awareness that the Convention had not been devised with the interests of small and poor countries in mind. Ever since, the country has loyally gone along with all international changes in intellectual property, without ever questioning whether they were in its interest.

There is an intriguing footnote to the 1925 episode. The Cabinet records on the country's access to the Paris Convention contain a letter from one of the officials who had been on the mission to the Hague, to a colleague back in Dublin. In this, he writes about the excitement of flying into the airfield at Paris in foggy conditions, 'so that they had to put lights down to guide us in.' Why an aeroplane, and why Paris? The obvious way to travel between Dublin and the Hague at that time was to take the morning boat and train from Kingstown (Dun Laoghaire) to Euston, and then cross to Liverpool Street for the night train and ferry via Harwich and the Hook of Holland. But Croydon to Le Bourget was one of the first regular air routes in Europe, and a large detour on expenses via Paris so as to experience air travel was clearly too good a chance to be missed.

Indigenous industry

The contrast with Finland in the Irish approach to intellectual property is instructive, and indeed Ireland can probably learn more from that country's performance than from any other. Both of them have much the same population size, both got their independence at around the same time (and it both cases it was followed by a civil war) and before independence both had been very economically dependent on a single natural resource: cattle in Ireland and lumber in Finland.

Ireland has had better overall economic growth recently, but this is primarily due to foreign–especially American–direct investment. For this, it has had the advantage in terms of physical proximity, the English language, a common law system, earlier membership of the Common Market/EU and low taxation. On the other hand, Finland leaves Ireland standing in terms of indigenous industrial development. Starting with the export of raw timber, the Finns first learned how to add value by turning it into plywood, and then by making the machines which did this and other kinds of wood-processing. No comparable industries for adding value to Irish raw materials were ever developed here. The unfavourable contrast is especially evident at the present time in the high-technology area. Even if we leave Nokia out of it (and there is nothing as an entrepreneurial *tour de force* remotely comparable to Nokia in Ireland) Finnish firms produce three times more patentable inventions.

To be fair to the politicians, given the short time-scale of the electoral cycle there really was no contest between policies of inward foreign investment and of indigenous development. Foreign firms could produce jobs quickly, whereas indigenous ones could only do so well into the future, and much less certainly. Neglect of the potential of intellectual property was an aspect of that choice, and any opportunity of reversing it productively was ended by the U.S.-engineered TRIPs annex to the agreement which set up the World Trade Organization in 1994 (cf. Sell, 2003). In the negotiations for this, the pass was sold by Brussels bureaucrats who had poor understanding of the issues, and who, incidentally, hardly bothered to tell Dublin what was going on. This American success in itself reflects the growth of rent-seeking in the EU, as a former vice-president of the European

Investment Bank noted recently:

> One of the most remarkable shifts in European economic policy governance in the last decades has been the evolution from the 'social partners' approach to a lobby-influenced approach . . . Policy in Brussels thus has evolved from a European-encompassing institutions approach to a US-Style 'special interest' approach. In fact, US companies and lobbies in many cases have been able to play this system much more efficiently than their European counterparts (Nowotny 2004).

It is no coincidence that this development is associated with consolidation of belief (not only in Brussels) in the superior wisdom of a European super-state.

Public-private partnerships

Several Tribunals have shown how strong is the tendency for members of political parties to become creatures of rent-seekers who provide them with funding, particularly since the coming of television so greatly increased the costs of getting elected. The inevitable result has been replacement of entrepreneurs who can contribute to genuine long-term wealth creation, by individuals who know 'how to work the system.'

This is particularly evident at present in attempts to use public-private partnerships. On the face of it, there seems to be sense in bringing private money and expertise into carrying out projects of a kind on which the public sector has a long record of incompetently squandering money. However, Mr. Ahern himself has complained about the extent to which Irish business men want only profits without risk (which of course is rent). As he put it in the Dáil, the private sector's 'amazingly helpful' proposals in this regard 'were to the effect that if taxpayers took all the risk, if they were guaranteed the contracts and if they received good extensions on a number of basic points for borrowing, they would be interested in considering a cherry-picked list of projects'. To complete as good a description of rent-seeking in action as could be asked for, he added that 'it was regrettable that Irish firms were not prepared to take the level of risk that people in other countries successfully took in their involvement in PPPs.' (Dáil debates, December 17, 2003).

Another aspect of this kind of rent-seeking is that civil servants have shown themselves to be poor protectors of the public interest in negotiations with private sector entrepreneurs. Public sector employees, who can neither gain nor lose much as a result of any outcome, are no match for individuals who eat, sleep and dream the task in hand because they can gain so much from it. Rent-seekers have also found that civil servants to-day (in contrast to their predecessors in the early years of the State) are by no means immune to the prospect of another career after retirement.

Getting the laws right

If belief in the superior wisdom of the State were ever to weaken, a possible start to dealing with rent-seeking would be to set up formal arrangements within the civil service for achieving public objectives by getting the laws right, instead of intervening in the economy (see Kingston 2004). This would mean developing a small elite group in each Department whose only function would be to suggest how changed or new legislation could contribute to solving a particular problem, before any decision is taken about it. Such a group would provide specific alternatives to the measures of intervention which the mass of the civil service could be counted on to continue to favour.

In Britain, a tentative step was taken in this direction in Lord Rothschild's Central Policy Review Staff, known as the 'think-tank,' in the Cabinet Office. Rothschild's brief to the CPRS was to 'think the unthinkable.' This was not popular with Departmental bureaucrats, whose influence helped to persuade Mrs. Thatcher to put an end to the experiment. An Irish angle to the work of the CPRS was that they took up an idea which had been generated but ignored here and turned it into the Business Start-up and Expansion Schemes, which provided tax relief for investment in non-quoted firms (Cabinet Office, 1978). When John Bruton was Minister of Finance, he wanted to copy what had by then become a considerable success in Britain, but the IDA resisted because they feared it would reduce rent-seeking firms' dependence on them for grants. However, Bruton got his way and BES schemes are still being operated in Ireland.

New Zealand example

Another potentially good model for this country has been the transformation of the New Zealand civil service. This resulted from the crisis of Britain's joining the Common Market, which demanded a complete re-orientation of policies. Although Irish civil servants have visited New Zealand to find out how this was done, it is unlikely that they will recommend the radical changes they found there, such as the replacement of lifetime employment with single-year contracts, which is one of the key elements in the outstanding contemporary efficiency of the New Zealand corps. Instead, any attempts at reform will continue to be based on the assumption that the civil service could be made more efficient by mimicking private sector practices.

Conclusion

Indeed, the likelihood of any kind of change for the better in the country must be low, when a former senior civil servant can list amongst the systemic causes of Irish policy failures, 'the competency of Cabinet members, coordination failure (often referred to as 'lack of joined-up government') growing clientelism, increasing numbers of political appointees to important boards and quangos, back-tracking on freedom of information, and a form of opposition that often appears half-hearted' (Casey 2005). The same writer's observation that 'the much-vaunted Strategic Management Initiative did not even clarify the respective roles of [Ministerial] adviser and [Departmental] secretary-general,' confirms that the present tinkering with the system cannot work, just as nothing less than a change of course could have saved the Titanic.

In spite of failures piled upon failures which can be blamed on it, 'belief in the superior wisdom of the state' remains as strong as ever in Irish policy-making. It continues to underwrite rent-seeking as the norm for national business and the trades unions, and thus to render an indigenous economy based upon genuine entrepreneurship impossible. This makes prosperity very largely dependent upon inward foreign investment, which of course is equally largely outside the Government's control. The country's future is therefore irrevocably locked into policies of the United States, and the Irish economy will swim and sink in line with that country's external deficit.

REFERENCES

Acts of the Oireachteas (1930): Hospitals' Sweepstakes (Temporary Provisions) Act.

Cabinet Office (1978): *Industrial Innovation*, London, HMSO.

Casey, Michael (2005) former Asst. Director-General of the Central Bank, Irish Times, August 22.

Daly, M.E. (1992): *Industrial Development and Irish National Identity*, Dublin: Gill and Macmillan.

Keynes, John M. (1936): *The General Theory of Employment, Interest and Money*, London, Macmillan.

Kingston, W. (2004): 'An Alternative Agenda for Public Service Reform' *Administration* 52 (1) 35-45.

Landes, D. (1970): *The Unbound Prometheus*, Cambridge: Cambridge University Press.

Liebenau, Jonathan (1988): *The Challenge of New Technology*, Aldershot, Gower Publishing.

McCague, E. (1994): *Arthur Cox.* Dublin: Gill and Macmillan.

Manning, M. and McDowell, M. (1984): *Electricity Supply in Ireland*, Dublin: Gill and MacMillan.

Muller, D. (1989): *Public Choice 2*, Cambridge: Cambridge University Press.

Nowotny, E. (2004): 'Evolution of Structures of European Economic Policy.' *Journal of*

Evolutionary Economics 14/2, 211-215.

O'Halpin, Eunan (1989): *Head of the Civil Service: a Study of Sir Warren Fisher*, London, Routledge.

O'Hearn, D. (1993): 'Global Competition, Europe and Irish Peripherality.' *Economic and Social Review*, January.

Sell, Susan K. (2003) *Private Power, Public Law: The Globalization of Intellectual Property*, Cambridge University Press.

Skidelsky, R. (1995): *The World After Communism*, London: Macmillan.

Synon, M. (1970): Unpublished M.B.A. Dissertation, Dublin: Trinity College.

Usher, D. (1981): *The Economic Prerequisite to Democracy*, Oxford: Blackwell.

Chapter II
The Lemmings of Democracy
(First published 1976)

Introduction

Marx said contemptuously of parliamentary democracy that it was only 'the committee of the bourgeoisie'. Today we are desperately at grips with the question: 'Can it ever be anything else?' Consider first an obvious contrast - between the country where democracy works most and best, and those countries where it does not work at all.

Nowhere are public affairs run through the ballot-box more than in Switzerland, where not just questions of foreign loans, but even issues such as the lengthening of the runways at Geneva airport can be the subject of a referendum. But even without crossing the iron Curtain, to where political choice does not exist at all, all the countries of Africa where the Colonial powers left one-man-one-vote quickly replaced it with some form of authoritarian regime. Consulting the electorate is as much of a sham in the third world as it is everyday reality in Switzerland, and the contrast is no less stark because of Swiss unwillingness in the past to give votes to women, nor of the existence of a large group of foreign workers who do not have the franchise there.

Next, consider a second contrast between Switzerland and the same countries, this time in terms of wealth. The differences are not so much in terms of total wealth - Nigeria is now also extremely rich because of oil, for example - but of the kind of wealth and the way it is distributed. In no country in the world are property and incomes so independent of the State as in Switzerland; there is widespread belief in market forces (as a corollary of which ownership tends to be widely distributed) and the owners of this property have shown themselves to be highly capable of generating real new wealth. In the ex-Colonial countries, wealth depends almost completely on the State; it is highly concentrated and linked to government corruption; and it has no evident power of generating further real wealth. Even where the oil riches of Nigeria, for example, spill over into private ownership, it is as a result of individual or family connections with the State machine, which effectively controls virtually all the national income. In Switzerland, on the other hand, the State's proportion of national income is only one-fifth - vastly lower than even in any other European country.

These are extremes, but whether one looks at them or the countries in between (the U.S. closer to Switzerland; Ireland, with the State share closer to Italy) there is no escaping the correlation between the two contrasts. Democracy is a property system. It can be seen to work where it is a counterweight to property, giving power to numbers *qua* numbers, to balance the power which property that is independent of the State must always possess. It can be seen not to work if it is introduced where there is little or no independent property which needs to be counterbalanced, and - what is the vital question now - it ceases to work if the amount of property to be counterbalanced is reduced, or if it becomes less independent of the State, with the power of numbers remaining undiminished.

Schumpeter's diagnosis

Correlation is not necessarily cause, but in this case the way in which democracy developed as part of the vast extension and expansion of wealth in Western civilization was convincingly demonstrated a generation ago by Joseph Schumpeter.[1] From this analysis, it is clear that Marx was perfectly right to sense that democracy is part of bourgeois achievement, but then, as Schumpeter also observed, no writer has ever been so much aware of 'what that achievement was and what it has meant to humanity,' as Marx.[2] Everything points to Schumpeter's thought being one of the most important moulding forces in coming years, as his work is seen to be increasingly prophetic and relevant to the questions which we now face. One of these is the relationship between democracy and property, in terms of both correlation and causality, and the lines of intellectual battle can now be seen to be drawn between those who see democracy as part of a balanced system, workable only in so far as, and for as long as, numbers act as a counterweight to a primary source of power, and those who think they can do away with property to a lesser or greater extent and still enjoy the benefits which democracy confers. It is probably not unfair to say that this second group includes Marxists, most Socialists, and not a few Liberals.

This is in line with the historical evolution of democracy. It is altogether a travesty of this to think that the counterweight of the franchise (the power of numbers simply as numbers) is something which has only been wrung by violence or, even more, by the fear of violence, from those with the primary power of property. At least equally, the record shows, there is a sense in which it can be claimed to be the conscience of Property, which has prevented the owners of wealth from using its power solely in their own interest; so much has democracy's

---

[1] Especially in *Capitalism, Socialism and Democracy* (1943)

[2] In *Journal of Political Economy* (1949) 209.

evolution owed to men who could, had they wished, have had their hands on the levers of the primary source of power but who devoted themselves to developing the counterweight to it. The 'Public School' contribution to the British Labour Party is only one example.

True private property

In the 'property-numbers' balance it is not just property in which title is invested in individuals that matters, but the extent to which such property is genuinely independent of the State. Obviously, the very first condition that requires to be fulfilled for this is that the wealth has not come about because of the State's direct administrative action. This is not just because it is in this area that the opportunities exist for corrupting politicians and public servants, but because those who make money in this way do so by conforming to an economic pattern and a set of objectives which are set by the Government. Since these can only reflect the 'numbers' side of the balance, property which exists only by conforming to them is a mediocre counterweight. It could even be that it is a misnomer to call wealth which has this origin private property at all, even though it is individuals who have title to it; rather is it an extension of the State apparatus, a form of public property given into private hands.

Next, it also seems necessary, for property to be an effective counterbalance to numbers, that it should not depend exclusively either upon the State's interference with market forces through the legislation which makes partial monopolies possible. The Companies' Acts, the Industrial Property (especially Trade Marks) Acts, and every Act that brings about restraint of trade (even when the objectives are undoubtedly good, such as laws controlling the establishment of Banks, entry to the Professions, or the sale of alcohol) are of this type. For every such Act enables money to be made in the form of economic rent, as a result of the power thus granted by law to escape the constraints which the market seeks to impose.

Whether or not this always involves 'exploitation', as Joan Robinson was concerned to prove in her famous book,[3] is unimportant for the present discussion, because what matters is that those who own property which has this origin, are beholden to the State machine and to that extent are unable to act independently of it. Their property is therefore a counterweight to numbers in the democratic balance only in a limited sense. This is underlined by the change in the type of person who is a typical owner of wealth in such a system. Just as in an inflationary situation those who survive are the money-manipulators rather than the producers of goods (this was a major factor in the hatred of Jews in Germany

---

[3] *The Theory of Imperfect Competition* (1933).

after the inflation of the 1920s) so in a society whose economic life is character-ized by monopoly, the owner of wealth is typically a *rentier*, whose money has come easily and who is not respected in any way for possessing it.

Even more, such people even lose belief themselves in a system which makes them wealthy by these means. Gibbon's first three chapters clearly express his view that in the later days of the Roman Empire the owners of property (which by then was overwhelmingly of the type that depends upon State administrative action) would not fight to protect it, as if they saw its spurious nature. In our own days Schumpeter called attention to the way in which 'the bourgeois order no longer makes any sense to the bourgeoisie itself, and that when all is said and nothing is done, it does not really care.'[4] It does seem that property that is truly private, that is independent of the State, and that men will fight to preserve, will invariably be found to have been achieved under the discipline of the market.

This is one reason why men who actually work the land have always clung so tenaciously to it; no economic activity historically has been so much subjected to market forces as agriculture. Where the market is operating, money is made by labour, risk and foresight, and men feel they have justly earned it; it is where there is State administrative or other action that disrupts the market that there is the 'quick buck', the big 'killings', opportunities for financial manipulation, and, above all, rich men with no conviction that their wealth is deserved. If, parallel with this, much power is given to numbers simply as numbers, there is nothing for this power to balance against and democracy must run riot. When that happens, as Aristotle pointed out, the outcome inevitably is that mob rule (ochlocracy) prevails and is then replaced by tyranny.

Balance unstable

It is very easy to see, then, why Switzerland can operate such a highly democratic system (there is a lot of property that is independent of the State, and therefore an effective balance) and why the ex-Colonial countries cannot have one at all (private wealth depends virtually completely upon State administrative action, so any weight to numbers would overwhelm it). It is also easy to find examples of extra weight being given to the 'numbers' side of the balance to maintain some kind of equilibrium with property, and therefore economic and political effective-ness, over a period when wealth was increasing., The Reform Act of 1832, the further extension of the franchise to universal male suffrage in 1867, the curb on the power of the House of Lords in 1910, are all intelligible as increases in the force numbers would be enabled to bring to bear, corresponding to the prodigious

---

[4] *Capitalism, Socialism and Democracy*, 161.

growth in real wealth in nineteenth-century Britain.

In contrast, there seems to be no case where a decline in real private wealth has been accompanied by a deliberate restriction of the power of numbers so as to maintain equilibrium, and the consequent effectiveness of a democratic system. The lowering of the voting age to eighteen, coming as it did in Britain and Ireland when property independent of the State was actually declining, was in fact a move in the opposite direction. There is nothing automatic about the equilibrium upon which a democratic system depends, and indeed there is an innate tendency in such a system towards self-destruction because of the way in which the power of numbers can be used to erode independent property.

The vote market

This in fact has happened in Western democratic States several times during the twentieth century. The destruction of independent wealth in Germany by the inflation after the first world war made the operation of Weimar democracy intrinsically impossible and an authoritarian regime was thus made inevitable. In France, what General de Gaulle castigated as 'the nefarious regime of the Parties' was a system where there was more democracy (i.e. more weight on the 'numbers' side) than the amount and distribution of 'independent' property in that country could stand. As his partial cure, the Presidential system of the Fifth Republic gives less weight to numbers as such than the Parliamentary system did - and France's political stability, coupled with her recovered prosperity, is evidence of the effectiveness of the better balance.

At the present time it is the capability of Britain to survive as a democracy that is increasingly being questioned, because of the way the balance has been shifting to 'numbers'. The most perceptive observers of what has been happening to democracy in Britain rely heavily upon Schumpeter's ideas.[5] Events have provided strong evidence of the power of these ideas to predict, and in the social as well as the natural sciences this is still the only test of sound theory. He pointed out as long ago as 1943 that the only explanation of the actual working of democracy that made sense was that politicians offer policies to the electorate, competitively, in exactly the same way as businesses offer brands of goods competitively: A political party 'is not, as classical doctrine would have us believe, a group of men who intend to promote public welfare upon some principle on which they are all agreed,' but 'a group whose members propose to act in concert in the competitive struggle for power'.

---

[5] cf. for example, Samuel Brittan, 'The Economic Contradictions of Democracy' in *British Journal of Political Science*, April 1975.

There are, however, differences between 'dealing in oil' and 'dealing in votes' and one of these is crucial.

In the economic market the coin in which the chooser casts his vote - the money he pays for his purchases - is also the resource, or at least a claim on the resources, which the supplier needs to continue and maybe to expand the process of supply. In the political market, while votes are the basis of power, they are not the material which power uses. The command over the resources of power comes from the taxing power which is awarded by a plurality of votes. There is no mechanism for ensuring that a plurality of votes implies a commitment by the voters of the quantum of resources required to fulfil the programme on which the winning political team has won an election.

The pure market-place requires the citizen to exercise his choice and to commit the resources required to fulfil it in the single act of purchase whereby he parts with his money.[6]

Suicidal rush

It is obvious, therefore, that the competitive battle for votes by parties can hardly be other than an auction of the use of the State's monopoly of force to shift resources from the 'property' to the 'numbers' side of the balance. As the bids in this auction become higher and higher, this has the progressive result that the amount of democracy a country can stand and still operate efficiently, is reduced. Since there is nothing in the system which will correspondingly reduce the power on the 'numbers' side to maintain a balance with the diminished 'property' side, the only possible outcome is that the system will accelerate towards less efficiency, especially in economic terms.

For a long time this process operated rather slowly; there was tacit agreement between Parties that certain things were not part of the auction; as long as the administrative class of the Civil Service tended to come from the side of 'property' rather than from 'numbers', the public bureaucracy was a moderating influence on policies; and the effect of the human losses of two world wars took time to be fully reflected in the average calibre of politicians. In recent years, however, the retreat has become a rout, the bids in the auction ever more frenzied, the erosion of property that is independent of the State machine more rapid, and the inefficiency of the system more intolerable.

Since all of these things reduce the amount of democracy a country can stand, the politicians who are responsible for them are making their own avocation increasingly obsolete, hastening the day when some form of authoritarian system of

---

[6] Peter Jay: *Employment, Inflation and Politics* (1976) 13.

government must replace them. In this apparent death-wish, their self-abandonment to the Party in its mindless rush for votes resembles the extraordinary migrations of the lemmings, those strange little animals of Norway, which are said to have as their only object their own destruction by drowning in the ocean.

Proportional representation

If this process has gone far in Britain, it could be expected to have gone even further in Ireland, since the Irish electoral system gives more weight to numbers than the British one does. Consequently, for it to work well, it would need to have relatively more independent property as counterbalance, but in fact the opposite has been the case. The private wealth that has come into existence in Ireland since the foundation of the State has very largely arisen out of the State's administrative action, and therefore does not weigh heavily as a counterbalance to numbers. Farmers too, have become progressively more dependent upon the State for their incomes and so count for less than they did.

The Irish combination of single transferable vote and multi-seat constituency gives far more weight to numbers as numbers than the straight vote in single-seat constituencies does. This is primarily because it puts candidates in a position of subservience to the electors that is abject in comparison with their position under the straight vote. An elector with a transferable vote can do the maximum possible harm to a candidate who displeases him by giving his vote to another candidate from the same Party. Under the straight-vote system, to do the same would force the elector to vote also for another Party, which he will be loth to do. Because of the power which an electorate with transferable votes thus wields over individual candidates, all those who stand for anything other than what 'numbers' want are filtered out of the political process and the exercise of independence by the politicians that get through this filter is rendered virtually impossible.

Secondly, under the transferable-vote system the number of seats won corresponds much more closely to the number of votes cast than results from the straight vote with its 'winner-take-all' results. Since in any market situation there is a basic tendency for participants to share equally, such a correspondence of seats with votes makes significant majorities impossible, so any government formed as a result is once again incapable of doing anything which would cause the withdrawal of the small amount of the support of 'numbers' which is essential for being able to stay in office. Every seat is effectively a 'marginal' seat, and any Party with even a few seats can hold the balance of power.

Thirdly, since the cabinet is formed from politicians, these characteristics are carried through to the Executive, so that a 'P.R.' cabinet is intrinsically less capable of standing up to the electorate's wants (however damaging these may be to the true interests of the State) than a 'straight-vote' cabinet. It is ironic, indeed, that the man who bears the style and title of Taoiseach (significantly, with his Deputy, the only office in the State for which the Constitution does not designate an equivalent in English) with its echoes of Führer and Duce and the disciplining of a feckless people to make the trains run on time, has in reality less power to lead his electorate anywhere than his counterpart in London who can only call himself First Lord of the Treasury.

Inadequate Ministers

All too often in Ireland the process of negative natural selection by the transferable-vote system has produced Ministers who are poorly equipped to cope with their tasks or with their civil servants, whose recruitment pattern inherently favours the extension of State power. They have equally been unable to control in any remotely effective fashion the Semi-State bodies which they have set up. These have established direct communication with the electorate through their Public Relations budgets, and so still further spancelled the politicians in their own regard. Even the discipline of servicing capital has been progressively abandoned. In terms of effect on the property weight of the democratic system, the results are evident, as between Ireland and Britain: the residual private sector in Ireland is significantly smaller (and also has less independence of the State); public borrowing is relatively far higher; the country's inflation rate is significantly higher than Britain's and there are even fewer signs of any will to correct it, and so on.

The destruction of the democratic balance in Ireland has been accelerating rapidly, and has followed an easily understandable sequence. Governmental action which initially eroded property made the system less capable of satisfying economic expectations; further governmental action to fill this gap was inevitably inflationary; since inflation is the abandonment of money, as one of the greatest of all human inventions, making money corresponds less and less to generating real new wealth, so the gap between expectation and reality widens again. The pattern is evident in many other countries but can be seen especially clearly in Ireland. Indigenous industry was progressively forced to operate in an economic climate in which it is impossible to innovate and invent competitively, so expanding and giving more employment. Where the State stepped in directly it invariably failed, since State-owned corporations have never, anywhere, shown themselves capable of innovating, and hardly ever, indeed, even of competing in conditions that are at all free. Consequently, Irish Governments turned to the multinational corporations for the innovation, the foreign exchange earnings, the investment and the employment which they had made it impossible for locally-owned industries to produce. The growth of the State sector in mixed economies, in fact, creates by far the most fruitful environment for the spread of the multi-national Corporation, and this type of firm is now the prime means whereby countries with more economic freedom—the home countries of the multi-nationals—are enabled to exact tribute from those which are less free.

Unfulfillable expectations

Another factor that has been of particular importance in Ireland has been the growth of the mass-media, financed by advertising. This intensified economic expectations just at the time when government policies were making the local economy less capable of satisfying them. It has also eliminated equality in misery as a political option. For, as long as the mass-media can report how people in the world's freer economies live, the desire for a Western standard of living must be in conflict in Ireland with the desire for an East European form of economic organization. In the attempt to evade the fundamental incompatibility of these two desires, Government involvement in the economy has been intensified to the point that the end of democracy itself is now clearly in sight.

Although in Britain thoughtful people are concerned with the parallels to Weimar, there is yet no sign of the emergence of any equivalent of the Nazis, nor is there fear of Westminster being burnt down. But in Ireland the existence of a body of men, organized and trained in killing for political ends, who cannot fail to be the beneficiaries of economic collapse, is only too obvious - and not least to the politicians. The existence of the IRA has seemed to strike panic into their efforts to destroy the property 'weight' of the balanced system in which they operate, and measures which can only extend the proletariat are paralleled by increasing terror of it. This is exactly in line with the process which Carlyle described in the early chapters of his French Revolution. Draconian security measures are a corollary of deficit financing.

Can anything be done to prevent the extinction of both independent property and democracy? There is no way in which the market for votes can be made to work as the markets for goods do because there is no way of building in the constraints that are automatic in the latter. All that can be done, therefore, is to restrict the area within which Government economic policy can operate. Parliamentary democracy worked well as long as it dealt only with a part of life and a part of the economy; it can only work again if it brought back to being one component of a balanced system - and this can only mean Government relinquishing many areas of its current involvement.

Constitutional constraint

There is no mechanism at all for this in Britain, where Parliament is supreme. Mr. Peter Jay has suggested that an independent tribunal be set up to take control of the money supply out of the hands of politicians, pointing out that the United States and West Germany, where this has been done, have much lower inflation rates. To the extent that inflation is a pernicious destroyer of the property-numbers balance, such a tribunal would be a step in the right direction. Ireland has a written Constitution which contains express commitments to both private property and democracy and therefore at least an implied commitment to the balance upon which simultaneous existence of both depends. However, the Constitution denies itself the power to prevent the Legislature from destroying this balance. The primary instruments of the erosion of property to the advantage of numbers are Finance Bills, which the President is specifically prohibited from referring to the Supreme Court for review of conformance to the Constitution. Money Bills, however, may be referred to the people by a provision which permits the President, if petitioned by a majority of the Senate and one-third of the Dail, to refuse to sign a Bill until there has been either a Referendum on it or a General Election. Just how weak a safeguard this is for the present need will be obvious when it is recalled that the demography of the Senate is now hardly distinguishable from that of the Dail, and that in both the disadvantages of Proportional Representation, referred to earlier, are paramount. When the issue at stake is precisely the excess weight of numbers in relation to property, appeal to 'the people' is hardly likely to redress the balance.

In the end, the question of whether democracy can survive or not comes down to whether or not there is some externally imposed constraint on the market for votes which fulfils a corresponding function to the constraints which are automatic in other markets. In the past this was supplied by factors such as the education and social class of legislators and civil servants, by received ideas, and by the influence of organized religion. Today, when the need for such a constraint is all the greater because of the effect of institutionalized forces for raising economic expectations, we must look elsewhere for it. In the Irish context, giving the Supreme Court power to review money bills may be crucial for the continuation of any form of democratic system. The function of a written Constitution, and of its interpretation by the Judiciary, is precisely to apply fundamental checks to the legislative arm. If there was ever a case for such constitutional constraints, surely this is it, when the lack of any automatic discipline in the market for votes must inevitably lead the legislature to steps which can only result in the overthrow of the Constitution itself.

There cannot be the slightest doubt that in Ireland today the balance between public and private economic activity, and the extent to which all life has become politicized, no longer correspond at all to the State as the Constitution prescribes it. The Constitution provides for laws to delimit the rights of private ownership (themselves 'antecedent to positive law') so as to 'reconcile their exercise with the common good'. However, the onus should be on the State to prove that any law which excludes private ownership in any area of economic life (e.g. electricity generation and distribution or the running of scheduled bus services) or which involves massive interference with the unequal distribution of income that is intrinsic to a private property system (i.e. any modern Finance Act) corresponds to this provision.

It could be extremely difficult for any Irish Government to sustain such a claim on the record, apart altogether from what is known of the history of democratic constitutions in other countries, when the balance between property and numbers has been destroyed. The evidence that the public good has not in fact been served by Finance Acts which provide for three-fifths and more of national income to be under the control of the State, in terms of unemployment, State debt, and the huge widening of the gap between Ireland and freer and richer countries, in spite of increasing hand-outs from these, suggests that these Acts are 'unconstitutional'.

It may seem altogether fanciful to envisage a test case in the Supreme Court, and be harder still to imagine the immediate effects of a decision by the Court against a Finance Act. The nearest analogy is with the revolutionary decisions of the U.S. Supreme Court on racial segregation. But democracy is such an evident prize, and so much better a way of enabling social change to take place than any alternative, that a people and a Supreme Court which had been made aware that it cannot be had without independent individual property, might decide that both were worth maintaining and that an explicit limit upon the amount of national income the Legislature might properly dispose of, was necessary.

In deciding the level of such a constraint, it is no argument against the Court that its members are unlikely to have any expertise or training in economics. It is professional economists who bear much responsibility for the State's financial and administrative gluttony. In particular, it was disciples of Keynes who called the attention of the higher civil service to the apple marked 'power without responsibility' on the tree of knowledge. Professional expertise is not what is required to be able to say whether an effective balance between property and numbers, and thus the very continuance of the State in its constitutional form, is being maintained. The proportion of national income which the Irish State can

handle directly without undermining democracy is obviously vastly less than it is
now, but whether it should be twenty per cent, thirty per cent or even thirty-five
per cent, is a function of the weight to numbers given by the electoral system at
any particular time, and upon how much 'independent' property there is. It is this
broad general judgment that the Supreme Court, in its function of reviewing legislation, is designed for, and that its members are equipped to make. For example,
borrowing to cover deficits on current account, or even on Capital account that
does not earn a proper return, means living now at the expense of future genera-
tions. It is not economic expertise that is needed in weighing up the issues at stake
in such policies.

Lord Hailsham has recently argued that Britain has no chance of escaping to-
talitarianism unless the absolute sovereignty of Parliament is ended. His remedy
is a written Constitution, but Irish experience shows that this is of little value in itself. The O Dálaigh affair made it quite clear how readily such poor checks as the
Irish Constitution provides at present are brushed aside when power is at stake.
If these checks are to be strengthened, a beginning must be made with Article 45,
which makes the Oireachtas the sole arbiter of how the State's 'social objectives'
are to be achieved, and which stands across the path of any attempt by private
citizens to call in the Courts to redress the balance of power. Any amendment of
this article ought to be supported by enabling the President to refer Money Bills
to the Supreme Court. And a third necessity is some extra-Parliamentary means
of initiating Constitutional change (in Switzerland, again, 50,000 signatures can
bring about a Referendum on anything).

It is the lack of this last measure which makes it virtually certain that no
change will in fact take place that could save the Legislature from itself and from
the Executive in economic affairs. At present, the only means for initiating a
change in the Constitution is through a Bill in the Dail. Since the problems have
arisen precisely because politicians would not discipline themselves, why should
we expect them to initiate any action which would impose an external discipline
on them? It is far more likely that for the sake of getting or keeping power, for
however short a term, they will continue to destroy the balance between independent property and numbers, until the resultant economic collapse brings about
the final extinguishing of democracy and with it their own role. The prospect may
sadden, but it should not surprise: once they are on the move, nothing can divert
the lemmings from their blind and headlong progress, and there does come a time,
after all, when they finally reach the sea.

Chapter III
Why Ireland failed to keep up
(First published 1994)

A National Economic and Social Council Report has discussed how poorly Irish long-term economic performance compares with that of five other small European countries[1]. Their consultant, Lars Mjoset of Norway, argues that the cause of this poor record has been failure to turn new ideas of many kinds into concrete realities. The significance of this conclusion is underlined when it is recalled that inability to innovate was also a clearly identifiable element in the economic collapse of the Soviet bloc.

Countries compared

There can only be limited value in comparing Ireland to three of the countries in the Mjoset study - Austria, Sweden and Switzerland. Because economic innovation is nothing more than human creativity expressed in a particular way, the capacity for it reflects earlier social and artistic traditions. Austria is the core remnant of a great Empire and its people are heirs to deep and diverse cultural and even industrial traditions. Sweden is one of the oldest autonomous kingdoms of Europe and has some of the finest iron ore in the world on which to build an engineering tradition. Mjoset excluded Norway from his list for comparisons because it has oil, but Switzerland has hydro-electric power.

Denmark and Finland

Comparisons with the other two countries, however, are both valid and enlightening. Denmark's agricultural performance has been held up as an example to Ireland since Sir Horace Plunkett pioneered the co-operative movement here[2]. But most can be learned from Finland. Both it and Ireland were colonized by a powerful neighbour, which in Finland's case was Sweden. Finland also had a great famine, in which 7 per cent of its people died; both countries got their independence at around the same time; both then had civil wars; both are geographically disadvantaged for much international trading.

In both Denmark and Finland, what Mjoset calls 'a national system of in-

---

[1] Mjoset, Lars, 1992. 'The Irish Economy in a Comparative Institutional Perspective', Dublin, National Economic and Social Council.

[2] West, Trevor, 1986. *Horace Plunkett: Co-operation and Politics*, Gerrards Cross, Colin Smythe.

novation' amounted to import substitution directed at the plant and equipment needed to add value to their natural resources. Thus, not only did the Danes capitalize upon the Swedish invention of the cream separator by developing their agricultural co-operatives with their associated folk high-schools, they invested in related industrial manufacturing to such effect that to-day equipment for dairy processing is the largest single item in Denmark's industrial exports. They also developed a pharmaceutical industry based upon animal extracts, and became one of the world's largest producers of insulin.

The Finns moved from exporting raw timber, firstly to the manufacture and export of forest products with added value such as paper and plywood, and then to production of the machinery to make these products. They also made a virtue of their cold climate by developing rock engineering expertise which has enabled them to build sports stadia and shopping centres underground[3]. This was then extended to making drilling and blasting equipment, so that in some of these fields, Finnish firms lead the world.

Irish failures

Why was there nothing in Ireland to match Finnish achievement since the 1920s? Why did it take so long for large-scale meat-processing to develop in Ireland and why was a machinery and equipment industry never built on Irish agricultural production? If the Finns could turn their cold environment to their advantage, why could the Irish not learn how to do the same with their wind and ocean-wave energy? Why did so few businesses which were set up under the industrial protection legislation of 1932-4 survive?

To answer these questions, Mjoset makes much of the importance of emigration in Irish history, and refers to a speculation of the late Raymond Crotty's that since it was the strongest and bravest who left the country, the Irish gene pool may be lacking in whatever elements go to make entrepreneurs and risk-takers[4]. There may be something in this, because such people are important out of all proportion to their numbers for industrial development. There is no apparent lack of entrepreneurial ability amongst Irish emigrants. Moreover, within this group for a full century straddling Independence, the foreign missionary effort channeled so much creative energy into non-economic activity that there is a sense in which this was Ireland's 'national system'. There is nothing like it in any of Mjoset's 'comparison' countries.

---

[3] Saari, Kari (ed.) 1988, 'The Rock Engineering Alternative', Helsinki, Finnish Tunnelling Association.

[4] Crotty, Raymond, 1986. *Ireland in Crisis*, Dingle, Brandon Books.

W. W. Rostow observed that the forced exile of the Huguenots was 'the critical margin for economic 'take-off' which France denied herself in 1685.'[5] In relation to the Irish population the number of missionaries stands comparison with
the proportion of Huguenots who left France, so what are the implications of their
voluntary exile for Irish economic development? They were well educated, and
there is plenty of evidence that many combined outstanding bravery with organis-
ing ability[6]. It is possible that in a different psychological and social context, their
energies might have been directed towards entrepreneurship in Ireland.

Church influence

The more general influence of religion on Irish economic development, which
Mjoset touches upon delicately, is complex. Leaving the missionary aspect aside, it
probably was not great until well after Independence. For a century from Emanci-
pation, the primary secular concern of the Catholic Church was building churches
and schools. The funding and personnel for these came mainly from the prosperity of Irish farming. This was on a strongly rising trajectory from the Famine until
the end of the first World War, mostly from producing cattle to satisfy the rapidly
growing demand of the population of Britain for meat. Even the invention of
refrigeration, which opened up the resources of the southern hemisphere, did not
immediately damage this prosperity. In giving their money and their children to
the Church, Irish families received prestige in return, but it is not evident that any
element in this exchange would have made the sorts of contribution to economic
development that can be seen in contemporary Denmark or Finland. Part of the
reason for this may be a general tendency of hierarchically-organised religion to
encourage social conformity rather than individual effort to bring about change.
Tawney, developing Weber's thesis, argued that it was especially in Protestantism
that 'the idea of economic progress as an end to be consciously sought ... found a
new sanction in the identification of labour and enterprise with the service of God.
The magnificent energy which changed in a century the face of material civilization was to draw nourishment from that temper'[7].

The 'corporatist' version of Catholic social thinking had a strong influence
on the 1937 Constitution. Its stress on private property rights is undermined by
lack of any constraint on the State's power to tax and borrow for involvement in
economic affairs[8].

---

[5] Rostow, W.W., 1975. *How It All Began*, p. 188. London, Methuen.

[6] See, for example, Forristal, Desmond, 1990. *The Second Burial of Bishop Shanahan*, Dublin,
Veritas.

[7] Tawney, R.H., 1926. *Religion and the Rise of Capitalism*. p. 249.

[8] See Kane, Aidan, 1993. 'A Public Choice View of the Irish Constitution', *Studies* (Winter) pp.
459-67.

The Importance of Property Rights

This involvement, in fact, offers the best explanation of Ireland's poor relative economic performance. Lack of entrepreneurs, for whatever reason, is not enough on its own. The institutional structure is at least as important—it should be noted how foreign entrepreneurs like Brown of Brown-Boveri moved to establish businesses in Switzerland when the conditions were right. But in Ireland, institutions have never been conducive to economic innovation. From Independence, and emphatically from the Lemass era, these were largely shaped by credulity about what a State can do for economic development through intervention, or 'Industrial Policy'. The main reason why Ireland failed to keep up, therefore, is indeed the same as for the failures of the Eastern bloc.

Western countries are as rich as they are simply because they alone developed a system of property rights which directed human creative energy fruitfully into economic channels[9]. There is a persuasive correlation between economic innovation and institutional arrangements which give individuals autonomy to act freely within limits laid down by law: 'those economies grew fastest which were freest'[10]. Mjoset is right to note that failure to grow reflects inability to innovate, but he fails to conclude that the reason for this is everywhere the same: claims of market failure, resulting in the further claim that the State has to intervene in the economy.

Market Failure as Legal Failure

But markets are not part of the structure of the universe. They are man-made artifacts, the result of positive law, especially laws of property rights. Much market failure, therefore, is legal failure, which in turn is the failure of those with power to construct appropriate frameworks for market activities.

Consequently, there is an alternative to intervention, which is to make laws which generate effective property rights. Rights are efficient only to the extent that they force individuals to serve the public good in following their own interest[11].

Mjoset's report confirms for Ireland what everything that has happened in Eastern Europe and the former Soviet Union has already shown: intervention cannot compare with creative law-making as a policy for long-term prosperity,

[9] North, Douglass, 1981. *Structure and Change in Economic History*, New York, W. W. Norton Co.; and Rosenberg, Nathan and L. E. Birdzell, 1986, *How the West Grew Rich*, London, Tauris.

[10] Landes, David, 1970. *The Unbound Prometheus*, p. 19. Cambridge, Cambridge University Press.

[11] North, Douglass, 1990. *Institutions, Institutional Change and Economic Performance*, p. 92. Cambridge, Cambridge University Press.

because it misdirects human energies. As William Baumol has pointed out, entrepreneurship can be productive, unproductive or even destructive. Which it is depends largely upon institutional arrangements[12]. Unproductive entrepreneurship is intelligible in the 'rent-seeking' concept of Public Choice economics. This sees government intervention as generating rents which business men seek to capture so that the entire federal budget can be regarded as a gigantic rent up for grabs for those who can exercise the most political muscle[13].

'Rentepreneurship'

Energy expended in this way is lost to other objectives, and the pickings from rent-seeking are often easier than those from productive investment, and always easier than from innovation. Worse, the availability of government-generated rents changes the type of person who engages in investment-related activity from entrepreneurs to 'rentepreneurs'. Individuals who are good at handling the politics of rent-capture are less capable of dealing with investment in competitive business; whilst those who have the abilities appropriate to the latter are inhibited from acting where politicians and bureaucrats are involved.

This explains how often Irish firms, apparently successful at home, failed against foreign competition. It is also compatible with Crotty's genetic degeneration theory in that presumably the 'real' entrepreneurs who might have contributed to wealth generation in Ireland would tend to emigrate, leaving the field to those best able to capture State-generated rents from projects with poor economic returns. The idea of 'crowding-out' of private investment by the demands of government projects is well-known. The parallel 'crowding-out' of an even scarcer resource, ability to identify and act on investment opportunities, by providing temptations to go after rents generated, or to be generated in the future by the State, badly needs researching.

No Lobby for Law-Making

Laws which generate effective property rights are needed for 'a national system of innovation'. Such laws would prevent politicians from benefiting their constituents directly, they would ensure that bureaucrats could not exercise power without responsibility and they would remove from powerful lobbies the fulcrum which they need to exert leverage. Unfortunately, the devising and enacting of such laws has little attraction for the powerful groups which would suffer as a result.

---

[12] Baumol, William J., 1990. 'Entrepreneurship, Productive, Unproductive and Destructive', *Journal of Political Economy* Vol. 98, No.3, pp. 893-921.

[13] Muller, Denis, 1989, *Public Choice 2*, p. 243. Cambridge, Cambridge University Press.

But it is precisely these constraints that enable law to underwrite innovation. In contrast, intervention reduces the economic space within which freedom under the law applies, and consequently hampers the fruitful expression of human creative energy in business. However hard it may be for politicians and bureaucrats to accept, the reality is that their intervention makes innovation impossible. The most significant comment in Mjoset's entire report is that in all five countries with which he was comparing Ireland unfavourably, 'no national innovation system was constructed by deliberate decision or choice'[14].

There are three reasons for this. Firstly, intervention requires a public bureaucracy, which consequently sets a low upper limit to the level of creativity which can be applied to innovation. A bureaucracy can only run well on comprehensive information, but it is the ability to act in the absence of information that defines the entrepreneur and innovator. Keynes noted that what appears to be necessary for economic success is 'exuberant inexperience'[15].

Secondly, intervention closes whole economic areas to private initiative, by handing them over to publicly-owned enterprises, which are notorious for failure to innovate. In Ireland, for example, the Electricity Supply Board considers that its mandate 'does not encompass general research and development in the energy field', and its monopoly makes it pointless for anyone else to do so.

Thirdly, intervention damages competitiveness. It is only at the stage of the incremental changes that are made during the process of learning by producing, that money is made from innovation. Only anticipated profitable production can make investment in innovation rational. Intervention distorts this profit measure, channelling investment towards projects which are politically rather than financially rewarding. Organized labour in the public sector is able to ratchet up wage rates because the Government can tax and borrow to pay them. Tax rates also increase to remunerate debt incurred to pay for uneconomic projects and higher public sector salaries as well as higher social security benefits granted in exchange for votes. Each of these factors reduces the attractiveness of investing in innovation; in combination, they make it impossible. The measure of competitiveness is profitability, which was no more than 0.2 per cent on turnover for indigenous Irish firms in the leading sectors between 1983 and 1990[16].

---

[14] Mjoset, Ref. 1 above, p. 17.

[15] Keynes, J. M., 1945 'Memorandum to Cabinet, 18 March'. *Collected Writings* Vol. 24 p. 261. London, Macmillan.

[16] O'Hearn, Denis, 1993, 'Global Competition, Europe and Irish Peripherality', *Economic and Social Review,* January. His figures are from the Industrial Development Authority.

Credulity about intervention

It is probably difficult for those who run a State which has come into being through revolution to escape being credulous about what intervention can achieve in economic matters. Every revolution is an attack on an existing property-rights system, so that success will carry with it a predisposition to intervene, since the new State which results is the expression of the energy which displaced the former property-owners. Moreover, one stage of nationalism characteristically included an element of rejection of industrialization, whose logic seemed to point towards submergence of human values under the blind forces of world-wide 'free' markets.

Consequently, Ireland could scarcely have escaped the first stage of intervention in its economy, the era of industrial protection in the 1930s, when most of its semi-state bodies were founded. However, this early 'Industrial Policy' failed to produce internationally competitive firms or to raise the standards of skills, of craft and of the value placed on workmanship. This is all the more interesting when it is borne in mind that the three strongest economies in the world, the U.S., Germany and Japan, all got their start by protecting their infant industries. The lesson from Mjoset's work, too, is how the economies with which he compares Ireland became strong by starting with import substitution.

The most likely reason why protection did not work in Ireland was that the market was so small that any product granted a quota or tariff in fact became a monopoly. The 'rentepreneurs' who benefited from Government interventions consequently did not have to worry about either customers or competition. Innovation of any kind did not interest them - many of their plants were equipped with secondhand machines to produce the obsolete designs of British products.

After the abandonment of the protectionist experiment in the 1950s, the country made a real advance, primarily as a result of a legal change. Zero-rating of tax on export profits transformed the value of holding property in the form of manufacturing assets in Ireland. The associated interventionist system of grants was far less important as an incentive to investment from abroad, and was ultimately self-defeating. The existence of such grants, however, enables politicians to avoid having to shoulder the unpopular task of legislating about whatever hinders efficiency, entrepreneurship and innovation.

External Borrowing

The scale and harmfulness of the 'infant industry' type of intervention was followed by inept responses to the two oil shocks in the 1970s. When the OPEC countries could not absorb all the money they were making, they recycled the unspent revenues through the international banks. But these revenues, which had come out of countries like Ireland in the form of increased costs to businesses and individuals, did not come back to the same people - they were lent to Governments. It was particularly unfortunate for Ireland that this happened when an unsophisticated form of Keynesian economics dominated academic and civil service thought. As a result, the advice which politicians were receiving confirmed their own inclination to borrow and spend. This borrowed money never earned an adequate return, so the cost of servicing it is still a powerful brake on Irish competitiveness.

'Political Discretionary Income'

Borrowing has been increased still more to meet the requirement of matching transfers from the EU. But neither Brussels"funny money' nor Irish real money can contribute seriously to innovation because of pressures on politicians to spend both in highly visible ways on public sector projects, in their own constituencies as far as possible and virtually without regard for financial return. The scramble for such funds is fierce, because they provide 'Political Discretionary Income', which can be spent in these ways, since so much of the regular budget is committed in advance for national rather than constituency requirements[17].

Visibility is also high for the two-fifths of the EU funds which is spent on 'training', since this temporarily reduces the recorded dole numbers, but lack of jobs for those 'trained' means that these funds and their Irish counterparts are almost completely wasted. About another quarter is spent on 'infrastructure' projects - roads, sewage schemes and the like. These and projects such as the ubiquitous heritage centres, force up taxes through operation, maintenance and debt service costs. This feeds into wage levels that inhibit long-term productive investment, and cannot be compensated for by lowering the exchange rate because of the scale of the country's external debt.

There is far too little awareness of how harmful the EU money is in its present form. One promising means of using structural or cohesion funds would be to apply them to the reduction of employers' Pay-Related Social Insurance, where they would go straight towards lowering the cost of labour and so ultimately improve competitiveness, which is a necessary but by no means a sufficient condition for innovation.

---

[17] Kingston, William, 1994, 'What Economic Convergence Really Demands' in Urban, Sabine (ed.) *Europe's Economic Future: Aspirations and Realities*, Wiesbaden, Gebler Verlag

Democracy and Property Rights

Granted that the State sector has grown strongly in every country throughout the present century, why has this trend been more damaging in Ireland? The answer is the rules which govern Irish democracy. Mjoset does make some references to 'clientelism', which is endemic to multi-seat proportional representation. Of even more importance are the ground rules within which this operates. Democracy is a property system. Voting works as a counterbalance to property, giving weight to numbers simply as numbers, and the amount of its influence that any economy can stand and remain economically efficient depends upon the amount of property which is independent of the State. Usher has shown theoretically that unless a significant proportion of incomes is independent of the State even democracy itself cannot survive[18]. In contrast, the most successful way of assigning incomes other than by voting is through individual property rights, so that:

> somewhere between full public ownership of the means of production and extreme laissez-faire is a line that the liberal society cannot cross or a grey area within which politics becomes increasingly factious and unwieldy as the public sector expands, until eventually the liberal society dissolves into despotism [19].

There is unfortunately no shortage of historical and even contemporary examples of States which confirm and illustrate Usher's arguments.

Irish Imbalance

Since so much property in Ireland has been obtained directly or indirectly through politics, the country has a lower proportion of property that is independent of the State than any of the Mjoset 'comparison' countries. At the same time its multi-seat proportional representation voting system gives a heavier weighting to numbers than any other type in practical use. Consequently, Ireland has a much more democratic structure of representative government than is compatible with economic efficiency in its particular circumstances. This is the root, not just of inability to innovate, but even of a general incompatibility of State ownership and competent management which is shown by, e.g. Irish Shipping, the Insurance Corporation of Ireland and Aer Lingus. This diagnosis not only explains the profligacy of the country's modem public finance, it could have predicted it[20]. And it gets further support from the case of Italy. Faced with national bankruptcy, that country's electorate has voted overwhelmingly to abandon proportional represen-

---

[18] Usher, Dan. 1981. *The Economic Prerequisite to Democracy*, p. 16. Oxford, Blackwell.

[19] Usher, Dan. 1990. *The Welfare Economics of Markets, Voting and Predation,* p. 469. Ann Arbor, University of Michigan Press.

[20] Kingston, William, 1976. 'The Lemmings of Democracy', *Studies* (Winter).

tation almost completely, in a desperate attempt to discipline its politicians.

Unfortunately, the imbalance between weight to independent property and weight to numbers is so great in Ireland that it could not be rectified by moving to the 'first-past-the-post' voting system used in Britain, or even to one of the 'list' systems. Some more drastic relative reduction of the weight to numbers, or a correspondingly severe restriction on the power of Governments to tax and borrow, would be needed. In a country which is now conditioned to look to politicians for favours, and where there is also the nucleus of an alternative standing army, the reaction to either change could well be violent.

A Mild Shift in Direction

Nevertheless, if Ireland's relative decline is not to become absolute, a start, however modest, has to be made quickly to develop an alternative to the interventionist near-consensus. The gap between Ireland and other countries came about because the case for efficient institutional arrangements went by default. Such a start could be to appoint an Assistant Secretary in each relevant Government Department whose sole duty would be to develop proposals for ministers on how objectives could be reached by law-making rather than by intervention. One cannot be optimistic, however, that ministers would often accept their suggestions. The multi-seat proportional representation system is particularly incapable of producing political leadership that has both the intention and ability to withstand pressures to intervene. But at least politicians would be forced to choose for the first time, since at present they get no alternative advice to that from interventionist public sector elements and various lobbies, all crying 'market failure' far too early.

Civil Service Morale

There is another argument for establishing formal units within the Civil Service to put the case for law against intervention. This is that since no State can do without a public bureaucracy, it is of the highest importance that this should not destroy itself by involvement in activities beyond its capacity.

Not all of Lemass's civil servants were enthusiastic about his interventionist policies[21]. From the 1950s, however, credulity about what the State can do became characteristic of the Irish Civil Service. Wherever the veil of secrecy has been lifted, it has been seen to be involved in direct intervention in the economy at a low level of effectiveness. The Bovine TB debacle, the poor supervision of Irish Steel and Irish Sugar, the revelations of the Beef Tribunal and the comments

---

[21] Lee, Joseph, 1989. *Ireland 1912-1985*, p. 241. Cambridge, Cambridge University Press.

of the Dail Public Accounts Committee on the Kilrush marina reflect this, and in every case there is cause for concern. As a result of such failures and the consequent growing practice of appointing politically selected advisers to Ministers, morale in the Irish Civil Service has been weakened.

Intervention inevitably lowers this morale, because it asks Civil Servants to do things which others can do better. In contrast, formulating the detail of laws within which individuals acting in their own interest, are forced to serve the public good, is a task which only a public bureaucracy can perform.

Examples of Legal Changes

Some examples will illustrate the kind of issues with which officials in the proposed new posts might concern themselves:-

* Limited Liability for shareholders is a legal device without which rates of economic growth in every country would have been far lower than they have been. For it to work in any honest productive investment, there is no need for shareholder anonymity. Yet Limited Liability now also involves unlimited anonymity, with consequences and implications that are comprehensively illustrated in every aspect of the Greencore and Telecom affairs[22]. The result has been to direct entrepreneurial brainpower and energy towards financial manipulation and rent-seeking, i.e. towards making money without having to make things - and certainly not towards innovation.

* It was never right to extend legal immunity from actions for damage caused to third parties by strikes, to public sector Trades Unions. This in fact amounts to a new (and very inefficient) property right in certain types of employment. It has also been a factor in escalating pay and restrictive practices to damaging levels in the private sector. The correct law would copy that which applies to Federal employees in the U.S. These are denied the power to strike, but have 'pendulum' or 'final issue' arbitration for their pay and conditions[23]. In this, the arbitrator must decide entirely in favour of one party or the other - it is not permitted to 'split the difference' in any way. This forces the parties to converge in their bargaining positions, lest by looking for too much, they leave the arbitrator with no option but to decide in favour of their opponent. It also greatly weakens the ratchet effect on settlements that is inevitable with traditional bargaining, in particular by strength-

---

[22] Curran, Maurice, 1990. Report into Siucre Eireann etc., Dublin, The Stationery Office; and Glackin, John A., 1991, 1993. Chestvale Properties and Roddie Investments Ltd., Interim and Final Reports to the Minister for Industry and Commerce. Dublin, The Stationery Office.

[23] Lewis, R, 1990. 'Strike-free Deals and Pendulum Arbitration', *British Journal of Industrial Relations*, Vol. 28, p. 32.

ening the influence of those Trade Union leaders who are able to see further in their members' interest than the immediate pay claim.

* Any shortage of entrepreneurs in the population is very easy to solve at the present time. Singapore's prosperity is due to a combination of an appropriate set of property rights with an influx of Chinese entrepreneurs from Malaysia, where independence had put an end to their control of most of the businesses of pre-War Malaya. Now many equally entrepreneurial Chinese want to leave Hong Kong, and they are being offered passports by countries like Canada on condition that they invest a substantial sum in a business there. If Ireland were to do the same, this small immigrant group could also be of great importance in forging commercial links with China, which must become a huge market within the next generation. The revelations that Irish Government Ministers do give passports to foreign business men without any formal structure is one more confirmation of how excessively politicized doing business in Ireland is.

* Ireland took its intellectual property laws passively from an international system which is overwhelmingly biassed in favour of the most advanced countries. The lack of any attempt to develop indigenous laws is a major factor in the poor national innovation system identified by Dr. Mjoset. This is important in two ways: firstly, the technologies of the future will increasingly depend upon information, and correspondingly upon new types of intellectual property law; secondly, the European Court has ruled that this law still remains under the control of national governments[24]. In this vital area, therefore, unilateral action in its own interest (possibly along lines already suggested elsewhere for Ireland) is not yet closed off to any EU member state[25]. As this is in fact the last, best hope for the Irish economy, it deserves some additional comment.

Intellectual Property

Ireland has never made any serious attempt to suit itself in this respect, even though a series of studies since the 1970's demonstrate how great is the balance of disadvantage which membership of the international system has had for the country[26]. Given Japan's outstanding success in innovation, it cannot be without significance that over the period 1945-80 when that country made no less than 18

---

[24] See, for example, European Court of Justice 1987 Case 238: Volvo v. Veng.

[25] Kingston, William, 1987. 'A Patent System to Suit Ireland', *Irish Banking Review* (Autumn) pp. 21-30.

[26] Beginning with Murdoch, R.J.P., 1971. *Invention and the Irish Patent System*, Dublin, Trinity College.

changes in its Patent Law to suit its innovators, Ireland made just a single one, and that was to keep in line with international developments[27].

There are historical reasons for this inertia. The Irish Free State joined the Paris Convention (which regulates Patent and Trade Mark matters) purely as a gesture of assertion of political independence from Britain, before it even had any intellectual property laws. The Minister of Industry and Commerce subsequently said of such laws that 'the better thing is for us to legislate all that the Convention seeks to achieve'[28]. He and his advisers appear to have been totally unaware of the reality that the international system had not been brought into being to further the interests of small and poor countries.

The same attitude of dependency is evident today in Irish acquiescence to moves by Brussels to capture the power to grant all intellectual property rights. As an illustration of this, only a few in a million voters in the Maastricht referendum can have been aware that the third item in the package on which they were being asked to decide was not necessitated by the treaty at all. This item empowered the Government to ratify an earlier, quite independent agreement, the Community Patent Convention. It would indeed have been very hard for the electorate to know what they were or were not voting for. Item 3 on the ballot paper was not explained at any time in official informational material, and as late as referendum week, no copy of the relevant text was available for inspection even in the Patent Office library, nor could one be bought from the Government Publications Sales Office. That this measure was successfully slipped through is especially regrettable, because the implications of this Convention are wholly bad for a country like Ireland, which - above all else, and like the other peripheral countries of the EU - needs property rights which will benefit it selectively.

Test of EU Good Faith

Economic convergence of the rich and poor economies in the EU (which is an aspiration of the Treaty of Rome) cannot be brought about by financial transfers from rich to poor, but only by differential property rights between them. That is, law must make it more profitable to carry on some kinds of economic activity, above all, innovative economic activity, in the poor countries than in the rich ones. That this is anything but the case at present, is evidenced by the fact that new employment generated by firms from the European 'core' countries in Ire-

---

[27] For the Japanese figures, see Rahn, Guntram, 1983, 'The Role of Industrial Property in Economic Development: The Japanese Experience'. *International Review of Industrial Property and Copyright Law*, Vol. 14, No.4.

[28] McGilligan, Patrick, 1927. Senate Debates Vol. 9, Cols. 548,568.

land has never exceeded 300 in any year since 1980[29]. Readiness to accept such differential rights would be a far better test of the good faith of the 'rich' EU than any doubling of the structural funds or any level of 'cohesion' fund.

Would they pass this test? Experience up to now is not encouraging. The right to property includes the right to its fruit, so that taxation modifies property rights. This country's former unilateral zero-rating of manufactured exports for tax therefore contributed to a differential property rights regime here. Replacing it with a 10% tax rate in response to EU prompting, eroded an Irish comparative advantage. It significantly reduced the value of holding property here in the form of manufacturing capacity. Even if the structural funds were indeed to be used to reduce Employers' PRSI, they could not remotely compensate for this, and, as argued above, at present they actually do harm.

The effective transfer of most of the value of Ireland's fishing grounds to Spain and the ecological destruction of common lands in the West as a result of sheep headage payments, also show that 'Political Discretionary Income' from Brussels has been obtained at a ruinous cost. Official policy seems to be to acquiesce in any degree of EU centralisation provided that Ireland is 'compensated'. But the only form of compensation on offer is financial, when what is really needed is genuine 'subsidiarity' in terms of property rights. Irish intellectual property legislation, reflecting the same deferential attitude, confirms that the country is involved in an international system that is strongly disadvantageous to it.

The Outlook

If there is no change in direction, therefore, the long-term result of these elements of policy in combination, all of which reflect national preference for intervention by the State to economic freedom under the law, is easily foreseen. It can be nothing else than a country with a progressively improving 'infrastructure', but with correspondingly less reason in terms of industry and employment, for that infrastructure to exist at all. Commitment to intervention will finally have eliminated any possibility of developing 'a national system of innovation', with the organic growth and prosperity that could follow it.

---

[29] O'Hearn Ref. 17 above.

Chapter IV
Entrepreneurship or Rent-Seeking?
(First published 1995)

Introduction

This chapter begins with a brief discussion of entrepreneurship, showing that this is an activity that can only exist when individuals are free to act within a framework of law and private property rights. The second section deals with the alternative, collectivism, in which the State is no longer content to establish the conditions within which entrepreneurs can act on their own initiative, but insists on intervening directly in economic affairs. This generates 'rents' for those whom this intervention favours.

The consequences of collectivism are dealt with in the third section. Whether central planning and control is substantially complete (as in the former Soviet Union) or partial (as in 'mixed' economies) only affects the extent of the waste of resources and consequently, the speed with which an unviable economy will develop. This is because entrepreneurs (who know how to handle productive investment) are replaced by 'rent-seekers' who know 'how to work the system' so as to adapt the State's power to their own interest.

The fourth section shows how Ireland has always been collectivist, both in inclination and practice. Unlike the former Soviet Bloc countries, it has so far escaped having to face up to the consequences through borrowing and the availability of EU transfers. But its bureaucrats and rent-seekers will be of little use when these funds run out. This is why there is such an absurd and dangerous incipient campaign for yet more 'compensation' from Brussels in exchange for Ireland's joining in the EU common currency.

ENTREPRENEURSHIP : Creativity in Business

It was the great Austrian economist, Joseph Schumpeter, who baptised Adam Smith's 'undertaker' as 'entrepreneur', and the idea of the individual whose initiative is essential if factors of production are to be co-ordinated is central to his thinking. He saw entrepreneurship in terms of human creativity applied to economic ends:

> [W]henever the economy or an industry or some firms in an industry do something that is outside the range of existing practice, we may speak of creative response

41

... a study of creative response in business becomes coterminous with a study of entrepreneurship (Schumpeter, 1947, p. 150).

In his mind, this creative response has three essential characteristics:

It can only be understood after it has taken place, hardly ever before. It shapes the whole course of subsequent events and their long run outcome. And thirdly, it has much to do with the quality of available personnel, both absolute and relative, and thus with individual decisions, actions and patterns of behaviour.

Schumpeter did not stress the distinction between innovation and entrepreneurship, although each activity is best understood when related to the other. An entrepreneur can then be defined as an innovator acting in an area of life where the appropriate measure is money. Traders also operate in such areas, but what an entrepreneur does requires more creative input than trading. The special qualities of entrepreneurs have been identified in a range from 'gap-filling' and 'input-completing' capacities (Liebenstein, 1968) to exceptional skill in persuasion (McCloskey and Klamer, 1995).

The Role of Economic Institutions

Schumpeter's ideas about entrepreneurship were formed in the period before the first world war, in a liberal and individualistic world where business was typically done with little reference to 'the State'. In particular, the markets which entrepreneurs faced, did not arise as a rule from public purchasing or financing. There were exceptions, of course: firms in the arms trade, such as Armstrongs and Vickers in England, always had to sell to governments; and Bismarck's innovation of the first social welfare system in the world, shortly after the unification of Germany, provided valuable markets for that country's nascent health-care industry. Nevertheless, the paucity of such examples testifies to the extent to which the general pattern was one in which business men did not have to think of the government as a source of their revenues.

There are strong grounds, indeed, for believing that it is only in a context of free markets based on private property rights that entrepreneurship can exist at all. This is because a crucial distinguishing ability of an entrepreneur is to be able to act in situations where much theoretically desirable information is lacking. Keynes (1945) noted that what appears to be necessary for economic success is 'exuberant inexperience'. Part of this ability comes from possessing what Michael Polanyi identified as tacit knowledge, that is, knowledge that cannot be articulated, that exists only in use and can be attained only by experience of its use, and that is expressed in flair and intuition: 'We always know more than we can say'. The corollary, as the philosopher, John Gray, has put it, is that:

individuals are most likely to be able to deploy their personal tacit knowledge when they are least constrained by collective decision-procedures in which this knowledge is diluted or lost. (This is, perhaps, especially true of that species of tacit knowledge which is expressed in entrepreneurial insight). In order to be able to make the best of their personal fund of tacit knowledge, individuals need a domain in which they may act solely on their own judgement (and, of course, at their own risk). Such a domain is provided by private property in productive assets (Gray, 1993, p. 74).

Property Rights

Western countries are as rich as they are, simply because they developed a system of property rights which directed human creative energy fruitfully into economic channels (North, 1981, Rosenberg & Birdzell, 1986). Also, the empirical correlation between entrepreneurial activity and institutional arrangements which give individuals autonomy to act freely within limits laid down by law is highly persuasive in economic history: 'those economies grew fastest which were freest' (Landes, 1970, p. 19).

It is important to note that many different kinds of law can provide a fruitful environment for entrepreneurial activity, as long as the key element of private ownership is included. For example, most ownership of productive assets today is through shareholding in corporations. However, the twelfth century saw an astounding outburst of entrepreneurship throughout Europe on the basis of a quite different type of law. The Cistercian reform of the Benedictine Order grew to 500 abbeys within a single century, because these monks were the entrepreneurs and technologists of the age, innovating large-scale farming and metal-working, the use of water-power and widespread provision of financial services. All this was done on the basis of the absolute property rights of ancient Rome, which had been continued unbroken through the monastic tradition (Kingston, 1993, 1994a).

Markets, then, are not part of the structure of the universe, as libertarians tend to believe. They are man-made artefacts, the result of positive law, and they can be changed accordingly. But their essential condition is freedom of entry, and this in turn depends upon the existence of private property rights which confer the power of autonomous action on individual entrepreneurs.

COLLECTIVISM

However, since Schumpeter formulated his theories about entrepreneurship, they have been made progressively more irrelevant through the world-wide growth of collectivism, of which Robert Skidelsky has recently written with much perception:

Collectivism - the belief that the State knows better than the market and can improve on the spontaneous tendencies of civil society, if necessary by suppressing them, has been the most egregious error of the twentieth century. Its extreme manifestations were Communism and Fascism, but it was also seen in the authoritarian State-led industrialisation policies of many developing countries, and large traces have been evident in the industrial and social policies of most developed economies. My contention is that this belief in the superior wisdom of the State breeds pathologies which deform, and at the limit destroy, the political economies based on it (Skidelsky; 1995, p. xiii).

Inadequate Property Rights

There are many reasons for the growth of collectivism during the present century. Amongst the most important has been the inadequacy of the contemporary property rights systems. As John Stuart Mill pointed out, 'the laws of property have never yet conformed to the principles on which the justification of private property rests'(Mill, 1848). One of those principles is that private property 'civilises' self-interest in economic activity by forcing it to serve the public good. It is only to the extent that they do this that rights are efficient (North, 1990, p. 92). How to get efficient property rights has always been a problem, and it is the supreme problem of political economy in the post-Communist era.

Certainly, the pattern of property rights which developed over the nineteenth century was anything but efficient in this sense, however much economic growth it underwrote. The vast new wealth generated by the industrial revolution was highly concentrated, due to a combination of absolute ownership, new laws conferring limited liability on investments, unrestricted inheritance and low taxation, all combined with legal restraint on worker association for the purpose of generating countervailing economic power. It is hardly surprising, therefore, that those who were outside the circles of privilege could be persuaded by collectivist thinkers that State control of economic life would be in their interest.

The first world war showed that nations could operate through central planning in actual practice and not just in theory, and this experience was brought to bear again in every country in responses, such as the 'New Deal' in the U.S., to the Depression. World war II repeated the earlier extension of State involvement in the economies of all combatants, and after it came the age of Keynes and the 'managed capitalism' of his disciples. The oil shocks of the 1970s provided further opportunities for extending the role of the State, because when the OPEC surpluses were recycled, they did not go back to the firms and individuals from whom they had been exacted, but were lent to governments.

Pressures on Politicians

Two of the most important factors which contributed to the belief that 'the State knows better than the market', have been increasing pressures on politicians to be immediately responsive to a mass electorate, and a fundamental change in the demography of public bureaucracies. Nineteenth century politicians did not have to cope with universal suffrage, nor with the enormous costs of present-day election campaigns, and they did not depend upon politics for their living. Today's typical politician is a professional, for whom loss or gain of a seat or a majority is supremely important. Also, electorates and lobbyists have learned how vulnerable modern politicians are to pressures which have a bearing on either funding or votes.

These have combined to produce what is known as the political business cycle, for which the time horizon is the next election. The short-term interests of politicians therefore diverge from the longer-term interests of their electorates. A similar divergence of interest is evident in relation to information. Truth is in the interest of electorates; secrecy and the spread of 'good news' are in the interest of politicians. It is intervention, of course, which illustrates most clearly that the interests of politicians do not coincide with the public good.

Civil Service Changes

Even if it is politicians who decide on interventionist policies, these have to be carried into effect by public bureaucracies. A radical demographic shift in the civil services of the most important States played a significant role in the growth of collectivism. This began before the 1914-18 War, but becomes very evident after it. The 'old' civil services of Europe were typified by Schumpeter's description of the Prussian one as 'supremely efficient, totally incorruptible, altogether independent of politics' (Schumpeter, 1939, p. 346). By their preference for law over intervention, they were responsible for much fruitful legislation. The culture shared by nineteenth-century civil servants and business men was conducive to entrepreneurship, because it placed the emphasis on limited government; law and property rights were the means by which individual creativity could have an economic outlet.

Modern Counterparts

In contrast, their modern counterparts readily believe that the State knows better than the market. To them, expansion of the State machine has positive merit, since it generates promotion opportunities and the prestige that accrues to those who wield power. Interventionist policies coincide with self-interest, all the more because they are so easily 'sugared over with pretence of public spirit' (MacNeice, 1936).

In advising Ministers, the case for market forces operating within a framework of positive law will never be advanced with anything like the same energy as that for some form of intervention, since this will expand the bureaucracy. No 'market' approach is possible without creativity and imagination in constantly reshaping the legal structure. In turn, these depend upon subconscious energies and tacit knowledge that will be released only when an individual's own interest is at stake. When both 'interest' and 'demographic' factors are taken into account, it is not surprising that modern civil servants are as much in favour of intervention as their Victorian predecessors were against it.

RENT-SEEKING

The disease of collectivism damages countries in three main ways: by eliminating entrepreneurship; by increasing the role of the new bureaucracy; and, worst of- all, by causing divergence between the interest of those who run a country and the public good.

Eliminating entrepreneurship

There is no half-way house between running an economy through laws and running it by intervention. The 'mixed economy' is very far from being a free and competitive one. Because intervention invariably limits competition, it cannot avoid imposing increased costs on the economy as a whole, and the only possible source of funds to pay these costs is the entrepreneurial sector. The more intervention, the more costs, and the less the economic environment is capable of sustaining entrepreneurship. To the extent, then, that intervention or 'Industrial Policy' is adopted, politicians and civil servants are effectively turning their backs on the development of legal frameworks within which individuals, acting in their own interest within competitive markets, are forced to serve the public good.

Such frameworks do not come into being spontaneously; they are difficult to shape, and they can only come out of a political culture which has a strong belief in the value of limited government. But they are the essential environment for entrepreneurship, and to the extent that there is failure to develop and maintain them, entrepreneurs are being expelled from the economic system. Their place will be taken by 'rent-seekers'. The situation is even worse than as reflected in Baumol's (1990) claim that the wrong kind of rules can cause entrepreneurship to become unproductive or even destructive. In fact, collectivist rules actually change the kind of person who becomes involved in investment activity.

Public Choice Economics

The concept of 'rent-seeking' was developed by the Public Choice or Virginia school of economists. There are several technical definitions of rent, but what they all add up to is 'the financial results of restrictions on competition'. Since it is impossible for governments to intervene in an economy without causing such restrictions, all intervention generates rents. This changes the way in which money is made. In a competitive world, financial gain results from satisfying the demands of consumers or their intermediate suppliers better than others do; in a world where State intervention replaces competitive markets, money is made instead through becoming the beneficiary of the rents which intervention generates.

This does not mean just learning about and responding to what the State is doing; very often, it is the rent-seeker who actively stimulates the Government to make a particular intervention. The result, in the language of Public Choice, is that '[t]he entire federal budget can be regarded as a gigantic rent up for grabs for those who can exercise the most political muscle'(Muller, 1989, p. 243).

Dominance by Rent-seekers

To the extent that intervention becomes important in an economy, replacement of entrepreneurs by rent-seekers is inevitable. Individuals who are able to deal successfully with investment in competitive business, are inhibited from acting where politicians and bureaucrats are concerned, because they think in such different ways. On the other hand, those who are good at handling the political and bureaucratic dimensions of rent-capture, by definition do not want to have to deal with the kind of competition in which entrepreneurship flourishes, nor are they able to handle it.

In this process, entrepreneurs who can contribute to genuine long-term wealth generation must be progressively driven out by others who are better able to capture State-generated rents from projects with low (indeed frequently negative) economic returns for the community as a whole. The idea of 'crowding-out' of private investment by the demands of government projects is well-known, but the parallel 'crowding-out' of an even scarcer resource, ability to identify and act on opportunities to generate real wealth, is at least as economically harmful.

When the State turns to a policy of intervention, entrepreneurs are also replaced by bureaucrats. These can be regarded as a special type of rent-seeker, because all but a tiny fraction of their own remuneration is rent, captured out of taxation. On its own, this would make them a powerful influence for intervention, and unfortunately it is reinforced by a fundamental antagonism between them and entrepreneurs. They cannot share the same tacit knowledge, they operate according to quite different reward/punishment systems, and their scope for the exercise of creativity, and their attitudes to risk cannot be equated (Kingston, 1995). This antagonism also explains why the managements which benefit most from the various incentives which are the instruments of intervention are the ones in which the bureaucrats who administer the incentives see the best reflection of themselves and their values. There is affinity between rent-seekers, just as there is antipathy between rent-seekers and entrepreneurs.

Economic Consequences

All intervention consequently widens the area of poor decision-making, by increasing the importance of bureaucratic rather than innovatory firms in an economy, and by strengthening the bureaucratic element in all managements. Wherever direct government inducements are important to a business, the balance of influence in its management between entrepreneurs and 'organisation men' is tipped in favour of the latter. This is because they think like the bureaucrats who control the award of contracts or grants, and so have most rapport with them.

Intervention of course distorts the profit measure, channelling money towards projects which are politically rather than financially rewarding. Organised labour in the public sector is then able to ratchet up wage rates because of the Government's power to tax and borrow to pay them. Tax rates also increase because of the need to remunerate debt issued to pay for uneconomic projects and higher public sector salaries, as well as higher social security benefits granted in exchange for votes. Each of these factors reduces the attractiveness of entrepreneurial activity; in combination, they make it impossible. Having themselves produced the conditions where it is perfectly natural for those whose own money is at risk, to refuse to invest, the politicians and bureaucrats unite in the claim that the market has failed once again. Consequently, they feel called upon to intervene. Another opportunity for rent-seekers arises, and the true productivity of the economy is forced down a further notch.

Political Nemesis

No matter how rich a country may be, there is a limit to this process. In fact, Dan Usher has shown with convincing logic that unless a significant proportion of incomes are independent of the State, even democracy itself cannot survive:

> 'Whatever we assume, it turns out that the attempt to assign incomes by voting gives rise to consequences so unacceptable that the voting mechanism itself would sooner or later be abandoned' (1981, p.16).'

Assigning incomes by voting' means an economy of intervention and rent-seeking. Since intervention specifically makes incomes into rents dependent on the State, it is consequently undermining democracy, and the politicians who respond to pressures for intervention are actively involved in digging democracy's grave. In contrast, the most successful way of assigning incomes other than by voting is through individual property rights, so that, as Usher puts it:

> somewhere between full public ownership of the means of production and extreme laissez-faire is a line that the liberal society cannot cross or a grey area within which politics becomes increasingly factious and unwieldy as the public sector expands, until eventually the liberal society dissolves into despotism (Usher, 1990, p. 469).

There is unfortunately no shortage of historical and even contemporary examples of States which confirm and illustrate Usher's arguments. Every despotism in Africa began with a one-man-one-vote system, left by the departing Imperial power. Democracy is in fact another of the benefits of efficient property rights, and depends upon them. Voting works as a counterbalance to property, giving weight to numbers simply as numbers, and the amount of its influence that any economy can stand and still be economically efficient, depends upon how much property independent of the State there is.

Living on Capital

The fear must be that rent-seeking is a form of living on cultural as well as economic capital, and that Western countries are surviving, when the Soviet Union collapsed, for no other reason than that their stocks of both kinds of capital were so much greater. In some cases, however, capital may have been run down so much through adoption of intervention and rent-seeking that the process is now politically irreversible. In that case, even they could face the prospect that '[D]emocratic societies, as they now operate, will self-destruct, perhaps slowly but nonetheless surely, unless the rules of the political game are changed' (Brennan and Buchanan, 1989, p. 150).

'Changing the rules of the political game' can mean nothing else than abandoning intervention, clamping down on rent-seeking, and attempting to govern through laws which can underwrite competitive markets. However hard it may be for politicians and bureaucrats to accept, the reality is that to the extent that they espouse intervention, they are expelling entrepreneurs from the economic system and replacing them with unproductive rent-seekers.

Unfortunately, since it is one of the effects of collectivism that it causes the self-interest of politicians to diverge from the public good, devising and enacting such laws hold little attraction for them. Efficient property rights deny them the ability to benefit their constituents and lobbyists directly. They equally deny power without responsibility to bureaucrats and remove the fulcrum which rent-seekers need to exert leverage. It is in these very denials, in fact, that their greatest value is to be found.

IRELAND: NO COUNTRY FOR ENTREPRENEURS

It would scarcely have been possible for an independent Ireland to escape belief that the State knows better than the market. Those who run a State which has come into being through revolution can hardly be other than credulous about what intervention can achieve in economic matters. Every revolution is an attack on an existing property-rights system, so it is inevitable that success will carry with it a predisposition to intervene, since the new State is the expression of the energy which displaced the former property-owners. In Ireland, too, the world-wide trend towards collectivism during the most of the twentieth century, converged with a local tradition from well before independence, of looking towards government for economic initiatives.

The Cumann na nGael government vacillated between status quo and interventionist policies. On the one hand, they wanted to maintain free trade with Britain and parity of the currency with sterling, and they were prudent about public borrowing; on the other, they were influenced by the old Sinn Fein doctrines which had been articulated by Arthur Griffith, inspired by the teaching of the German economist, Friedrich List, on industrial development through protection for infant industries.

The beginnings of rent-seeking can be observed during this period, therefore, in numbers of applications for tariff and quota protection. For example, the successful lobbying for preferential excise terms by P.J. Carroll, the Dundalk tobacco firm, was so blatant a reduction of competition as to exclude their Belfast rival, Gallaher's, completely from the Free State market. It is also significant that at least part of the stimulus for setting up the first of the semi-state bodies the Shannon Scheme/ESB, was to pre-empt a private enterprise hydro-electric scheme on the Liffey (Manning and McDowell, 1984,pp. 1314, 28). One of the most striking examples of successful rent-seeking during this, or indeed any other period, was the Irish Hospitals' Sweepstakes, the specific legislation for which made it possible for a former Government Minister and his associates to amass very large fortunes (Dáil Eireann, 1930).

The Lemass era

A drift towards collectivism became a flood with the coming to power of Fianna

Fail in 1932. Indeed, it is not an unreasonable interpretation of Lee (1989, p. 241) that if Sean Lemass had had his way, the Irish economy might have become every bit as centrally controlled as any in Eastern Europe. Nothing illustrates the meaning of rent-seeking better than the lobbying to capture the advantages of the industrial protection then being offered by the Irish State. This was all the more in evidence because many of the protective arrangements were individually negotiated by Lemass, and indeed kept secret. (Daly, 1992, p. 110).

This industrialisation policy, of course, was not at all to the taste of de Valera, whose ideal was a rural society. It is highly plausible that he did not object because the other side of the coin of industrial protection was financial support for the political party he had founded. The accountants and lawyers who specialised as go-betweens (two firms in particular) also shared in the resulting rents (Daly, 1992, p. 179; cf. McCague, 1994).

These new businesses needed little if any entrepreneurship. All that mattered was the level of protection. The rent-seekers who benefited from Government intervention consequently did not have to worry about either their customers or competition. Innovation of any kind was certainly not on their agenda - many of their plants were equipped with second-hand machines to produce the obsolete designs of British products.

Parallel rent-seeking within the civil service can be illustrated from the careers of two Principal Officers in Lemass's Department. These were persistent advocates of a nitrogenous fertiliser industry, but invariably came up against Department of Finance evidence that this had no economic rationale whatever. Eventually, they obtained a promise from their Minister that if ever they could persuade other departments of the project's value, they would have jobs 'high up' in the proposed firm. The plant was eventually set up for political, not economic reasons (in what was possibly the most unsuitable site in the entire country because a seat had been lost locally); the civil servants became Chairman and Managing Director; and another continuing financial burden was loaded on to Irish farmers and taxpayers (Synon, 1970, p. 66).

Failure of Protection

Because they had so little creativity in them, the protected industries signally failed even to try to become internationally competitive, and they did nothing to raise the standards of employee skills, of craft and of the value placed on workmanship. After abandonment of the protectionist experiment in the 1950s, the country made a real advance, primarily, it should be noted, as a result of a legal change. Zero-rating of tax on export profits transformed the value of holding property in the form of manufacturing assets in Ireland. The associated interventionist system of grants was far less important as an incentive to investment from abroad, and was ultimately self-defeating. This was because grants are no more than capitalised subsidies to compensate for disadvantages of locating here. Their existence enables politicians to avoid having to shoulder the unpopular task of legislating about whatever is holding back entrepreneurship. This neglect allows the disadvantages to remain in existence; indeed, in some cases they grow to such an extent that in the end no possible level of grant aid can compensate for them.

Lessons from the Hyster Case

How self-defeating this aspect of industrial policy can be, is well illustrated by the case of Hyster. This U.S. manufacturer of fork-lift trucks and similar equipment played off the South of Ireland against the North, so as to get an exceptional grant for setting up a plant in Blanchardstown (the amount was so large that it could not be revealed). When this plant did not prosper, they approached the Industrial Development Authority with a proposal for another large grant, this time to enable them make spare parts in the large Limerick factory which a Dutch firm, Ferenka, had abandoned. This was of course welcomed, but Hyster then called attention to a difficulty: the parts they intended to manufacture were for their competitors' machines, not their own. A recent High Court ruling, following a British precedent, had given spare parts protection through the copyright in the drawings from which they were made. Hyster could therefore expect to be sued on this basis by competitors if they went ahead with their plan.

The Industrial Development Authority naturally lobbied on their behalf, and the upshot was a dramatic and urgent intervention in the Senate by the Minister for Industry and Commerce. At the time, an amendment to the Copyright Act, outlawing video nasties, was being discussed. The Minister insisted that a second amendment be added, overturning the Court judgment (which had related to fish boxes). The Government fell shortly afterwards, and the amendment lapsed with it. Hyster's Blanchardstown project collapsed and they left the country. Nonetheless, in due course the amendment came up again before a new Dail and Senate, and 'the proposed change in the law to facilitate the proposed Hyster factory in Limerick' (Dail Debates, 1987) was solemnly passed.

The subordinate position of law to intervention as means of achieving industrial development, in the minds of both politicians and bureaucrats, is very evident from this case. It is confirmed by the sequel. The British response to the judicial precedent referred to, was to introduce a quite new kind of functional design protection in the Copyright, Patents and Designs Act, 1988. This is particularly well suited to protecting the incremental innovations of the types of business which are common in Ireland (and could be made even more valuable if it included registration arrangements with Internet-type dissemination). The Irish authorities had an opportunity of copying this in the Patents Act of 1992, but opted instead for the now outdated German system of 'utility models' in the form of short-term 'patents' which are not examined, and consequently have no presumption of validity at all.

External Borrowing

The scale and harmfulness of the rent-seeking associated with the 'infant industry' type of intervention was unfortunately supplemented by what followed as a result of the two oil shocks in the 1970s. Recycling of the OPEC surpluses came at a particularly unfortunate time for Ireland, when an unsophisticated form of Keynesian economics dominated in both academic and civil service circles. As a result, the advice which politicians were receiving confirmed their natural inclination to borrow and spend. None of this borrowed money ever earned an adequate return (in fact, much of it went on greatly increased public sector pay) so the cost of servicing it will remain indefinitely as a brake on Irish competitiveness. This problem can only continue to worsen year by year, because the EU's 'monetary union' guideline for debt/GDP ratio - itself a particularly misleading measure in Ireland's case (Murphy, 1994) - has replaced a balanced budget as the accepted objective of policy.

European Union Funding

Borrowing has been increased still more to meet the requirement of matching transfers from the EU, which have further widened the field for rent-seeking. Politicians are under strong pressures to spend these funds in highly visible ways on public sector projects, in their own constituencies as far as possible and virtually without regard for financial return. The scramble for such funds is particularly fierce, because only they provide 'Political Discretionary Income', because so much of the regular budget is committed in advance for national rather than constituency requirements (Kingston, 1994c).

What escapes observation in respect of most EU-funded projects, many of which would never have been undertaken on a fully rational assessment, is the link - through operation, maintenance and debt service costs - with high taxation. This feeds through into wage levels that inhibit long-term productive investment, and these cannot be compensated for by lowering the exchange rate because of the scale of the country's external debt. Similar damage from structural and cohesion funding in other poor EU countries helps to explain why economic convergence will remain an unfulfilled aspiration of the Treaty of Rome (Kingston, 1994b).

A Harmful Voting System

Granted that the state sector has grown strongly in every country throughout the present century, why has it been more damaging in Ireland than in any other OECD country (cf. Mjoset, 1991)? Why, in particular, has Ireland's economic record been so much worse than that of Finland, which is otherwise so similar (Kingston, 1994c)? Much of the answer may be discovered in the country's electoral system. This is very effective at enabling individuals to bring their preferences to bear on politicians, who are almost defenceless against the claims of sectional interests, because neither the Constitution nor the prevailing social culture constrain Government powers to tax and borrow.

Since so much property in Ireland has been obtained directly or indirectly (by rent-seeking) through politics, the country has a very low proportion of property that is independent of the State. At the same time it has a voting system' (multiseat proportional representation) which gives a heavier weighting to numbers than any other type in practical use. (The property/numbers balance is exactly opposite in Switzerland which, significantly, is the richest country. Its frequent use of referenda also acts as a restraint on collectivist tendencies).

Consequently, Ireland has a much more democratic structure of representative government than is compatible with economic efficiency. This diagnosis not alone explains the profligacy of its modern public finance, but even enabled it to be predicted (Kingston, 1976). It is also the root cause, not just of an inhospitable environment for entrepreneurship, but of a general incompatibility of State ownership and competent management which is illustrated by the unhappy record of almost every one of the semi-state bodies.

The argument that there is a connection between the property/numbers balance, the electoral system and the strength of collectivism has received powerful reinforcement from the case of Italy. Faced with national bankruptcy, that country's electorate has voted overwhelmingly to change its voting system from proportional representation in an attempt to discipline its politicians.

Unfortunately, the imbalance between weight to independent property and weight to numbers is so great in Ireland that it could not be rectified just by moving to the 'first-past-the-post' voting system used in Britain or even to one of the 'list' systems. Some more drastic relative reduction of the weight to numbers, or a correspondingly severe restriction on the power of Governments to tax and borrow, would be needed. In a country which is now so conditioned to look to politicians for favours, and where there is also the nucleus of an alternative standing army, the reaction to either change could literally be explosive.

Victory of the Rent-seekers

Needless to say, so much 'unearned' money in the hands of politicians, whether from external borrowing or EU transfers, has been the target of a host of rent-seekers. These have been rewarded, for example, by special tax breaks (the Temple Bar area) legislation benefiting specific individuals (the Financial Services Centre) purchase of assets with public money at inflated prices (Telecom, the Kilrush marina) or disposal of public assets without competitive tendering (CIE), monopoly grant of export credit insurance (beef firms) and, of course, ubiquitous land rezoning (construction companies). Apart from the inevitable waste of resources which has resulted, several public enquiries have unfortunately provided evidence of how thin is the line between rent-seeking and corruption of the civil service as well as politicians. These include Curran, 1990; Glacken, 1991, 1993; the Beef Tribunal, 1993 (cf. especially O'Toole, 1994); and Committee on Public Accounts, 1994.

Indeed, the victory of rent-seekers over entrepreneurs in Ireland must now be considered to be virtually complete. In 1983-90, indigenous Irish manufacturing firms were only able to earn a rate of profit of 0.2 per cent on their sales (O'Hearn, 1993, p. 79). In 1994, in spite of all the employment-related subventions from the State, such firms could only add a nett 202 jobs. In the same year, again in spite of massive subsidies, there were only 11 more jobs in all manufacturing industry, both foreign-owned and indigenous, than in 1985 (Forfas, 1995). It is widely accepted amongst business men that total costs are £2,000 per worker-year higher in the Republic than in Northern Ireland, largely because of taxation differences.

These are no conditions to encourage entrepreneurial activity, and they compare most unfavourably with the relentless success of rent-seeking, both as indicated above, and in public-sector pay. A distressing aspect of the resulting imbalance is the increasing proportion of the population which is excluded from autonomous economic activity and dependent upon the State.

Last Chance in the EU Saloon?

Because EU guidelines are preventing politicians from borrowing as much as they would like, the continuation of the privileged position of the country's rent-seekers is now very dependent on transfers from Brussels. These are due to be reduced substantially within a few years, so it might be thought possible to hope for at least a limited conversion then to saner policies. It is not too difficult to identify changes in Company, Trades Union and Intellectual Property law which could produce a business environment much more conducive to entrepreneurship (Kingston, 1994c).

Some, however, are hoping instead for a last-ditch effort by the Government to obtain another round of EU funding to postpone having to face reality for a few more years. This would take the form of payments to Ireland to compensate it for difficulties in joining in the common European currency. For a country to claim that it is strong enough to join, at the same time as asking for compensation for joining, might seem the height of absurdity. Unfortunately, it fits in with a suggestion by M. Chirac that those who do not adopt the common currency should pay those who do. The logic of this argument is that by not over-valuing their national currencies, the countries which do not join would have an advantage in selling their products.

In the Irish case, then, it is not quite beyond the bounds of possibility that those who provide the EU with money, mainly of course Germany, would be willing to pay what by their standards would be a small amount for the sake of maintaining a vassal State in the North Atlantic world.

In that event, Irish credulity about the superior wisdom of the State would be sustainable in the interest of the rent-seekers who benefit from it, for just a bit longer. Sooner or later, however, Skidelsky's contention that collectivism destroys political economies is no less likely to be proved right in Ireland than it has already been in the countries of Eastern Europe.

REFERENCES

Baumol, W. J. (1990): 'Entrepreneurship: Productive, Unproductive and Destructive', *Journal of Political Economy*, 98(5): 893-921.

Brennan, G. and Buchanan, J.M. (1989): *The Reason of Rules*, Cambridge: Cambridge University Press.

Curran, M. (1990): 'Report into Siucre Eireann etc.', Dublin: The Stationery Office.

Dail Debates, 14 October 1987, Mr. Desmond O'Malley.

Dail Eireann, Hospitals' Sweepstakes (Temporary Provisions) Act, 1930. 30 per cent (7 per cent for any individual) of all revenues were allowed for the promoters' expenses.

Dail Eireann Committee on Public Accounts, 1994: Second Interim Report on the Report of the Comptroller and Auditor-General for 1991. Dublin: The Stationery Office (PN 0574). For rent-seeking, see in particular finding No. 11.

Daly, M.E. (1992): *Industrial Development and Irish National Identity*, Dublin: Gill and Macmillan.

Forfas Annual Report (1995): Dublin: The Stationery Office.

Glackin, J.A. (1991), (1993): Chestvale Properties and Hoddle Investments Ltd. Interim and Final Reports to the Minister for Industry and Commerce, Dublin: The Stationery Office.

Gray, J. (1993): *Beyond the New Right*, London: Routledge.

Keynes, J.M. (1945): 'Memorandum to Cabinet', 18 March. In *Collected Writings* 24, London: Macmillan: 261.

Kingston, W (1976): 'The Lemmings of Democracy', *Studies* 65: 297-309.

Kingston, W -(1993): 'Property Rights and the Making of Christendom' *Studies* 82: 402-425.

Kingston, W (1994a): 'A Reflection in Ganagobie', *Crisis* (November), Washington, DC.

Kingston, W (1994b): 'Economic Convergence: an Aspiration Unfulfilled', in Urban, S. (ed.) *Europe's Economic Future*, Wiesbaden, Gabler Verlag: 53-75.

Kingston, W (1994c): 'Why Ireland Failed to Keep Up', *Studies* 83: 251-264.

Kingston, W (1995): 'Innovation or Bureaucracy'? *Creativity and Innovation Management*, 5(3), September.

Landes, D. (1970): *The Unbound Prometheus*, Cambridge: Cambridge University Press.

Lee, J. (1989): *Ireland, 1912-1985*, Cambridge: Cambridge University Press.

Liebenstein,H. (1966): AEA Papers and Proceedings: 75.

McCague, E. (1994): *Arthur Cox*, Dublin: Gill and Macmillan.

McCloskey, D. and Klamer, A. (1995): 'One Quarter of GDP is Persuasion'. *AEA Papers and Proceedings*, 85(2): 194.

MacNeice, L. (1936): 'Eclogue from Iceland', in *Collected Poems*, 1966, London: Faber and Faber .

Manning, M. and McDowell, M. (1984): *Electricity Supply in Ireland*, Dublin: Gill and MacMillan.

Mill, J. S. (1848): *Principles of Political Economy* Book II, Chapter I.

Mjoset, L. (1992): *The Irish Economy in a Comparative Institutional Perspective*, Dublin: National Economic and Social Council.

Muller, D. (1989): *Public Choice 2*, Cambridge: Cambridge University Press.

Murphy, A. (1994): *The Irish Economy: Celtic Tiger or Tortoise?* Dublin: MMI Stockbrokers.

North, D. (1981): *Structure and Change in Economic History*, New York: WW Norton Co.

North, D. (1990): *Institutions, Institutional Change and Economic Performance*, Cambridge: Cambridge University Press.

O'Hearn, D. (1993): 'Global Competition, Europe and Irish Peripherality', *Economic and Social Review*, January. Figures quoted are from the Industrial Development Authority.

O'Toole, F. (1994): *Meanwhile, Back at the Ranch*, London: Vintage.

Rosenberg, N. and Birdzell, L.E. (1986): *How the West Grew Rich*, London: Tauris.

Schumpeter, J.A. (1939): *Business Cycles*, London: McGraw Hill.

Schumpeter, J.A. (1947): 'The Creative Response in Economic History'. *Journal of Economic History*: 152.

Skidelsky, R. (1995): *The World After Communism*, London: Macmillan.

Synon, M. (1970): Unpublished M.B.A. Dissertation, Dublin: Trinity College. Her information comes from interviews with Sean Lemass.

Tribunal of Enquiry into the Beef Industry (1993): Dublin: The Stationery Office.

Usher, D.(1981): *The Economic Prerequisite to Democracy*, Oxford: Blackwell.

Usher, D. (1990): *The Welfare Economics of Markets, Voting and Predation*, Ann Arbor: University of Michigan Press.

Chapter V
Innovation: New Property Rights are Better than State Involvement
(First published 1989)

Does more research and development (R&D) lead to a more competitive economy? By no means necessarily. The UK is close to the top of the R&D/GDP ratio league, yet it has a negative (and worsening) balance of trade in manufactures. The relationship between R&D and competitive products is complex, non-linear in effect, uncertain in the direction of causality, and every bit as weak as that between capital formation and economic growth.

In the late 1970s, for example, Irish investment in machinery and equipment as a proportion of GDP was significantly higher than Japan's, yet the returns on this investment during the 1980s for the two countries could hardly have differed more[1]. There is no reason to think that Irish spending on R&D has done any better. Interested parties regularly call attention to Ireland's relatively low rate of R&D spending by international standards, and demand that it should be increased. But in fact it is too high for the development of a competitive economy, because so much of it is controlled by bureaucrats in the employ of the state: the Japanese record alone is overwhelming evidence that for the development of competitive products, 'it is commercially funded and oriented R&D that correlates with commercial results'[2].

This Irish R&D expenditure pattern is merely one aspect of national credulity about the value of state intervention in the economy, or industrial policy. Three successive and overlapping waves of cash flows from abroad have both fostered intervention and postponed the growth of awareness that it does not work. Ireland in fact is a perfect example of how intervention results in an economically derivative society, characterised above all by inability to innovate. Dawning recognition of this during the last Government's term is reflected in the OECD's study of innovation policy in Ireland[3]. But this, being largely dependent, as these supranational documents are, on tendentious material supplied by local civil servants, proposes as a solution a series of initiatives that are bound to fail. This is inevita-

---

[1] OECD National Accounts, 1981.

[2] L. Franko, *The Threat of Japanese Multinationals*, Chichester: John Wiley 1983, 30.

[3] OECD, *Innovation Policy Ireland*, Paris: OECD 1987.

ble, because the report relies on continuing intervention to bring about the hoped-for results. It blames current difficulties on the fact that earlier interventionist policies were 'not sufficiently directed towards supporting innovation', not on the very existence of such policies. Its recommendations leave all the state agencies and apparatus in place (even calling for more power and responsibility for some of them[4], when what is needed is to replace them with new kinds of individual property rights that would enable creative energy to flourish in the economic field through decentralised decision-making.

MARKET FAILURE THEORY

Public financial support of R&D everywhere is the result of alliances between politicians who think there is a simple linear relationship between it and products that will produce money and jobs, bureaucrats who want power without personal responsibility, and academic scientists who simply want more money for research. Its record is one of consistent failure, which has often been spectacular[5]. It does not lead to competitive products, nor to economic growth through innovation[6]. Spending public money on science only tends to produce more science, not competitive products. And, where their effectiveness has been measured, subsidies to firms for R&D have not been justified by results[7].

The case for intervention rests on the premise that, left to itself, private enterprise will not do the 'right' things, or enough of them. This is because market forces direct private-sector activity to areas of lowest risk and quickest profit. Because of its high risks and long timescale, innovation is held to be a classic case of such 'market failure', requiring that the state step in to fill the gap.

This view, however, ignores the truth that real-world markets are not part of the structure of the universe, but are social artefacts. They are structures of positive law, especially in relation to property rights[8]. Much market failure, therefore, is in fact legal failure. Developing new kinds of law to generate an environment within which individuals acting freely in their own interest also serve the public good is always an alternative to intervention. It is one, moreover, with an

---

[4] Ibid., 67.

[5] See especially Professor David Henderson's outstanding BBC radio talks on 'The Unimportance of Being Right', published in *The Listener*, 27 October-24 November 1977.

[6] Richard R. Nelson, *High-Technology Policies: a Five-Nation Study*; Washington: American Enterprise Institute 1984.

[7] Stuart Macdonald, 'Theoretically Sound, Practically Useless?: Government Grants for Industrial R&D in Australia' in *Research Policy*; vol. 15 (1986), 269-83.

[8] William Kingston, *The Political Economy of Innovation*, The Hague and Boston: Martinus Nijhoff 1984.

unmatched record of success, since it is the evolution of property rights, more recently in relation to information, that has been primarily responsible for the innovation on which the world's wealth is based[9].

This is not to claim that everything can be left to decentralised decisions. But they have far more potential than they are being allowed to realise, because all three parties in the alliance that favours public support for R&D invariably raise the cry of 'market failure' too soon. They perceive, correctly, that the alternative - creative lawmaking - is arduous, gives no scope for empire-building, and produces less money for *fundamental* research.

The linear view of innovation

Because invention comes before innovation in time, it is often simplistically assumed that there is a linear progression from basic research to applied research to product development to products that can compete in the market. In fact, whether products are competitive or not is primarily a function of their market power, and scientific R&D may be no more than one component in one type of market power. Further, any linearity there is in the process of developing new products may often run backwards, i.e. from market intelligence to development to applied research and (very rarely and very modestly) to basic research. Spending public money at the R&D end in the hope of finding a fairy godmother at the market end (as the Irish state is currently doing through its new NBST-IIRS hybrid 'Eolas') is precisely the kind of public-sector fantasy that has led the country into a mire of debt.

However, the harm of having bureaucrats in charge of funding R&D is by no means limited to the cases where they are actually responsible for carrying out the research. It is also apparent when they administer grants to assist private firms to carry out R&D. Innovators and bureaucrats do not have mutual imaginative rapport (to put it mildly), so the firms that get grants inevitably tend to be those whose managements are most like the grant-givers. When intervention reaches the stage of replacing law to a substantial extent, as in the Irish case, it generates a dependent management class, incapable of innovation or of developing competitive products, irrespective of the amount of public money thrown at it. This has even begun to be recognised in Ireland, as what is called the 'grant mentality', but it has yet to be widely understood that it is an inescapable consequence of using intervention instead of law to achieve economic aims.

Belief in market failure is probably the deepest of all elements in the Irish view of industry and economics. Every revolution is partly against prevailing

---

[9] Douglass North, *Structure and Change in Economic History*, New York: Norton 1981.

property rights. Since the British system had contributed so much of the law that makes innovation possible, it was probably inevitable that, in reaction, the Irish should opt for a more collectivist approach. But there have been other factors. Politicians who are selected by multi-seat proportional representation are the least able of all to resist lobbies for intervention[10]. Irish senior public sector employees tend not to have family backgrounds in industry. The influence of Keynes, mediated by academic economists who, like their scientific colleagues, have been only too ready to tap a new and rich source of funding, has provided intellectual justification for policies that expanded the role of the state[11]. The Irish public sector is consequently particularly antagonistic to any development that would use law to enable decentralised decisions, about R&D or anything else, to be taken by business people on their own.

The BES and Hyster Cases

Tax relief on equity investment in private firms (the Business Expansion Scheme) is a case in point. The ideas on which the British government acted were available simultaneously to the Irish one, but were ignored[12]. The minister who eventually wished to follow British success with them met intense civil service opposition, so that the Irish copy is hedged around with restrictions, some of which are altogether absurd. For example, the relief was explicitly intended to take the place of state grants[13]. But in service industries it is only obtainable in association with an IDA grant, and this grant cannot be just for a feasibility study[14]. An incentive specifically intended to get investors to risk their money, therefore, is not available to them when the risk is highest, but only if and when it is lowered!

What happened in the case of Hyster is perhaps even more revealing. An Irish judicial decision followed British precedent in extending copyright protection to functional objects. According to this, copying a three-dimensional object infringes the artistic copyright in the drawings from which it has been made[15]. The resulting new type of protection showed itself to be extremely valuable for the types of innovation most suited to smaller firms. This was recognised in Britain, to the extent of establishing a new 'unregistered design right' by statute[16]. In Ireland,

---

[10] William Kingston, 'The Lemmings of Democracy' *Studies*, Autumn 1976.

[11] William Kingston, 'Ideas, Civil Servants and Keynes' in *Economic Affairs*, January 1983.

[12] Advisory Committee on Applied Research and Development, 'Exploiting Invention', London: Cabinet Office 1980, section 25.

[13] OECD, *Innovation Policy Ireland*, 58.

[14] Finance Act, 1984, s. 16 (2) (a) (ii).

[15] British Leyland v. Armstrong Patents Ltd. in the UK; Alibert v. O'Connor in Ireland.

[16] In the Copyright, Patents and Designs Act, 1988.

however, Hyster, a multinational favourite of the IDA, proposed to take over the former Ferenka factory in Limerick to make spare parts for competitors' products. The judge-made law blocked this, since these competitors would be able to claim infringement of their original drawings for the parts. A rushed amendment to the Copyright Act was introduced to remove this legal obstacle, in total disregard of its negative effect on the capacity of indigenous firms to innovate - a capacity that the State claims stridently is its policy to encourage! The final absurdity was that after Hyster's collapse and departure from the country, the amendment to the law that had been introduced to facilitate them, and for no other purpose, continued onwards through the legislative process![17].

But if intervention cannot enable the country to realise whatever capacity it may have to innovate competitive products, neither can the existing property rights structure. Of the many changes in this that are needed, the one with the most immediately beneficial effect would undoubtedly be to introduce direct protection of innovation along the lines recently studied for the EC by international experts[18]. Its particular implications for Ireland have also been briefly examined[19].

Ireland became involved in the international patent and trade mark system by subscribing to the Paris Convention in 1925. By doing so it bound itself to treat the nationals of other member-countries in the same way as its own for patent purposes, in exchange, of course, for the same 'national treatment' from them. Although joining the convention resulted in quite new and important property rights of exceptional value, it was never discussed by the Dail, by the Seanad, or even by the Government[20]. Its consequences were completely neglected both by politicians and bureaucrats, hell-bent on intervention as they have progressively been since then. But empirical research in TCD has demonstrated what a bad bargain for the country it turned out to be[21]. The international system gives all the advantages to the firms that are at the very cutting edge of all technologies, of which Ireland does not possess a single one. For every £1 of royalty it has brought into the country, at least £100,000 has gone out. Nor has the patent system con-

---

[17] Dáil Debates, 14 October 1987. Mr Desmond O'Malley: '. . . the proposed change in the law to facilitate the proposed Hyster factory in Limerick.'.

[18] William Kingston (ed.), *Direct Protection of Innovation*, Dordrecht and Boston: Martinus Nijhoff 1987.

[19] William Kingston, 'A Patent System to Suit Ireland?' *Irish Banking Review*, September 1987.

[20] All the government minutes for 1925 have been examined, without trace.

[21] H. J. P. Murdoch, *Invention and the Irish Patent System*, Trinity College, Dublin, Administrative Research Bureau 1971.

tributed materially to inward foreign investment, except possibly in the case of pharmaceuticals[22].

Direct protection of innovation

Adding arrangements to protect innovation directly to the existing system could do much to redress this imbalance. It would link the grant of protection to local investment. It would ensure that all R&D was done with wholly commercial objectives. It would direct resources towards those who can use them best in innovation, instead of those who have affinities with the bureaucrats who administer any system of public financial aids to industry. Above all, it would stimulate incremental innovation, and innovation of products and components of products that the classical patent system fails to protect.

These are both areas in which Irish industry could hope to be profitably involved. There are countless opportunities in them, in respect of which the first country to introduce direct innovation protection will get a head start. In spite of the Single European Act, such an option is open to individual states of the Community because of article 36 of the Treaty of Rome. Articles 30 to 34 are those that provide for a Community-wide market, unimpeded by national restrictions. However, article 36 derogates from these in respect of industrial and commercial property, provided that this is not used as 'a means of arbitrary discrimination or a disguised restriction on trade between member-states'. In 1982 the European Court confirmed in respect of designs that, because of article 36, 'in the present state of Community law and in the absence of Community standardisation or of a harmonisation of laws, the determination of the conditions and procedure under which protection...is granted is a matter for national rules'[23]. The same ruling was extended to patents by the court in 1988, and amplified in two ways that are important for direct protection of innovation[24]. Firstly, the fact that national and foreign applicants are equal before the patent law was held to dispose of the question whether the discrimination was arbitrary. The same equality is included in the proposals for direct protection of innovation. Secondly, the court held that the objective in legislation 'to foster creative activity on the part of inventors in the interest of industry' saved it from being 'a disguised restriction on trade between member-states'. The whole object of direct protection of innovation, of course, is just such fostering.

---

[22] Patrick Collins, 'Is the Patent System Relevant to Foreign Investment in Ireland?' (unpublished MBA dissertation, TCD) 1982.

[23] Keurkoop v. Nancy Kean Gifts (case 144/81).

[24] Thetford Corp. v. Fiamma SpA (case 35/87).

These rulings by the European Court confirm that the way is open for the introduction into national laws of direct protection of innovation. If objection were to be raised from any source, the further argument that direct protection of innovation was doing no more than bringing one aspect of intellectual property (the patent system) back to its origins would also have to be considered seriously by the court. Professed readiness to extinguish a national system as soon as direct protection of innovation was introduced on a Community-wide basis would also presumably carry weight with the court, as evidence of restriction of intent to fostering creative activity.

Political interest in Ireland in this idea reached the stage of a proposal to introduce a private member's bill to put it into effect. If it ever became law, it could provide an immediate boost to Irish competitiveness. However, in themselves these new property rights can only ensure that investment and effort are not deprived of rewards by the actions of 'free-riders'. They need to be complemented by arrangements for backing ideas with money. This can never be a rational activity. Uncertainty, not risk, and failure, not success, hold sway here.

Nor can these drawbacks be overcome by a portfolio approach, in which a spread of risk results in a few successes paying for many failures. There is persuasive empirical evidence that at the 'ideas' stage, the wider the range of a portfolio the worse the results are likely to be.[25] The rich individuals who so often provided seed capital in the past were able to do so largely because they had no way of knowing how high the odds against them were, but the growth of accountancy and risk analysis techniques has changed all that. Direct public funding of the early stage of innovation has never worked, because what is difficult enough for those who are spending their own money is impossible for an employed investor who is spending someone else's. And, as could be expected, those whose careers are at stake demonstrate remarkable ingenuity in devising means of avoiding backing ideas[26]. The situation is not quite hopeless, however, and a radically new approach to this problem that has recently been advanced in an international context has special attractions for countries such as Ireland[27].

United States 'SBIR' programs

By far the best source of seed capital in the world at present is the American Small Business Innovation Research Act, 1982. Recognising the wastefulness of public

---

[25] W. D. Nordhaus, *Invention, Growth and Welfare*, Cambridge (Mass.): MIT Press 1969, 55-6.

[26] William Kingston, 'The Financing of New Businesses' in *Industrial Innovation*, London: HMSO for the Cabinet Office 1979.

[27] William Kingston, address to the Institute of Patentees and Inventors, in *Future*, April 1988.

sector R&D, this forces federal agencies that are involved in it to divert part of their budgets (to the extent this year of no less than $400 million) to smaller private firms, in a three-stage competitive award system. In the first instance, awards of $50,000 for six-month feasibility studies go to about one applicant in nine. Second-stage awards, made to about half of the first-stage winners, can be up to $500,000 for two years' work. The third stage is where private venture capital is intended to take over, and in fact prior conditional commitments for such funding are taken into account in the second-stage assessment.

There is an overwhelming case for copying the Small Business Innovation Research (SBIR) scheme in Europe, but it is essential that this be done at the Community, not the national, level, if it is to reach the necessary critical mass[28]. What national governments could do, however, is adapt the SBIR approach to the distribution of funds obtained by increasing the level of fees charged to keep patents and trade marks in force.

In Ireland these are about £1.3 million annually for patents and £0.7 million for trade marks, and at these levels the office covers its costs and passes over about £1.5 million a year to the State[29]. Demand for maintenance of valuable monopolies must be highly inelastic, so that trebling these fees could be expected to produce an additional £3 to 4 million a year to begin with, for a new seed capital fund. More than 99 per cent of this would come from foreign-owned firms, reflecting the extent to which Irish patent and trade mark monopolies benefit them rather than local firms. The financial institutions might be persuaded to match this amount, for two reasons: firstly, much managerial time is spent at present in 'evaluating' proposals that are at far too early a stage to be bankable, and this, together with associated bad debts, could be saved by automatic referral of all such projects to the new fund; and secondly, success of some of the projects will generate demand for conventional finance in the future.

A welcome by-product for the banks could be an end to harangues from politicians urging the merit of taking unjustifiable risks with their depositors' money.

A 'seed capital' fund

The Government could also fairly contribute the £1.5 million a year it receives from the Patents Office in return for the vastly greater savings it would make by cutting out public funding of research. Since the 'research' stage of projects is inexpensive compared with what comes later, the resulting total of about £8 mil-

---

[28] William Kingston, 'Community R&D Funding: the U.S. shows a Better Way', in *European Affairs*, Winter 1988.

[29] Report of the Controller of Patents and Trade Marks for the Year Ending 31 December 1986, Dublin: Stationery Office (PL. 4962) 1987.

lion a year, properly used, could hardly fail to lay the foundations for a significant improvement in the competitiveness of Irish products. The fund could pay for the production of prototypes and for subsequent development work on them, on the SBIR model of competitive awards.

Although the money available to the fund would not be raised through taxation (no firm has to keep its patents in force, and brands are protected by common law as well as by trade mark registration) it would still be public money, albeit 'diverted'. Consequently, special precautions would have to be taken in the arrangements for its distribution to avoid 'interventionist' values returning by the back door. All decisions about ideas have to be taken on the basis of information that is no better than pre-quantitative, even pre-semantic.

'Meetings of imaginations' are therefore all-important, and the element of peer review, which is standard practice in the natural and social sciences, should dominate the making of awards.

In this context, the 'peers' of applicants would not be bureaucrats or bankers but individuals with actual experience of success (and failure) in innovation. Any committee of such individuals should have a rapidly changing membership, so that ideas can be exposed to the widest possible range of imaginations by repeated applications over a fairly short period. The fund should operate constantly on the basis of objective and invariably published research into its own effects (which would be in sharp contrast to the behaviour of the state bodies). And finally, since in an imperfect world any money-distributing agency is in danger from bureaucratic empire-building, its proportion of administrative costs should be pegged to the level of charities that are known to be efficient.

Conclusion

Irish enthusiasm for intervention, continued in the face of a record of failure that should have discredited it long ago, is due largely to default. It is not enough to condemn its results without at the same time putting forward practical alternatives in the form of more sophisticated property rights. The two proposals outlined above do this, by offering very much better and virtually costless replacements for some aspects of science and industrial policy. In addition to their specific contribution to improving the productivity of Irish R&D, their successful adoption would show how other aspects of the economy might also be set free.

Chapter VI
What Can We Do About the Civil Service?
(First published 2001)

An aspect of recent revelations from Tribunals and other enquiries is how badly the Civil Service has come out of them. What has emerged is much less to do with financial corruption (although there has been that also) than with failure to perform the tasks assigned to different Departments to any level of reasonable expectation. There is no need to rehearse these sorry stories; instead, it is useful to try to answer two questions, firstly, why is the performance so poor, and then, can anything be done about it?

Civil service origins

All public bureaucracies go back to the Papal Civil Service of the medieval Church, via the *ministeriales* of regional magnates (originally serfs selected for administrative and military purposes who thereby acquired the status of petty nobles). Several of those in Europe were modernised during the nineteenth century. One of Napoleon's greatest legacies to France was the Grandes Ecoles, the group of specialist schools he founded to provide technically-qualified administrators for the State. This greatly reinforced the institution of the Civil Service 'family' as a recognisable sociological entity in France. Not long afterwards, Hardenberg's reforms opened the Prussian Civil Service to all social classes, to build a corps on ethical foundations which had been laid by Huguenot immigrants and that could later be described as 'supremely competent, utterly uncorruptible.' In Britain, the Trevelyan-Northcote reforms of the mid-century made civil service recruitment depend upon competitive examinations instead of nepotism and achieved enviable standards.

Independence of employment

A feature common to all these 'older' bureaucracies was that they were class-based, with members having a degree of independence of their jobs through either private means or alternative careers. They depended upon 'a social stratum of adequate quality and corresponding prestige...not too rich, not too poor, not too exclusive, not too accessible' (Schumpeter 1943 p. 294). This social stratum, however, was destroyed by World War I. In both Germany and Austria, war casualties were compounded by post-war hyper-inflation, which of course completely undermined its economic basis. Many French Civil Service families just disappeared. In Britain, where the chances of surviving the war as an officer were six times worse than as a private soldier, the cohort which would have staffed the higher, policy-making posts in the Civil Service of the inter-war years was virtually wiped out on the Western Front (cf. Kingston 1983). Those lost had to be replaced by people who were totally dependent on their jobs.

What this demographic change meant is dramatically illustrated by some comments by Nevil Norway (better known as Nevil Shute, the novelist) on the loss of the British Airship R101. Its construction was a Labour party prestige project, and had been given a strict deadline by the Secretary of State for Air, who committed himself to fly to India in it. Throughout, it was beset with technical problems and it never completed its flight trials. Nevertheless, the day before it was due to depart, civil servants were prevailed upon to give it a certificate of airworthiness. This also turned out to be the death warrant of the Secretary of State and his entire entourage, as the airship had only got as far as Beauvais before it crashed in flames.

Norway, incidentally the son of the civil servant who was in charge of the Dublin GPO in 1916, was a remarkable engineer who had first-hand knowledge of the story, and wrote about it:

> The high executive civil servants at the top...appreciated that quite abnormal and unjustifiable risks were being taken with R101...they failed to speak up against Lord Thompson because they were afraid... If just one of them had stood up at the conference table when the issue of the certificate of airworthiness was under discussion and said - 'this thing is wrong and I'll be no party to it. I'm sorry, gentlemen, but if you do this, I'm resigning' - if that had been said then or on any one of a dozen previous opportunities, the disaster would have almost certainly been averted. It was not said, because the men in question put their jobs before their duty.

> Perhaps it is easy for an engineer to write like this, because he can get another job without much difficulty in some other branch of engineering; perhaps it is even easier for an author. This should not blind us to the facts, however, that in this case a number of high civil servants shirked their duty to preserve their jobs. It may be that under modern conditions of life in England it is unfair to expect a man who has spent his life in government service and is unfitted for any other occupation to place his duty to the State before his job. But if that be so, it should be clearly recognised that in certain circumstances these high civil servants will not do their duty, though all the honours in the book be showered on them by the Crown... I think this is an aspect of inherited incomes which deserves greater attention than it has had up till now. If the effect of excessive taxation and death duties in a country is to make all high officials dependent on their pay and pensions, then the standard of administration will decline and that country will get into greater dif-

ficulties than ever. Conversely, in a wealthy country with relatively low taxation and much inherited income a proportion of the high officials will be independent of their job and the standard of administration will probably be high (Shute 1954 pp. 138, 151-2).

Irish conditions

What Norway described as 'modern conditions of life in England' have in fact always been the conditions of Irish civil servants, and it is consequently unrealistic as well as unfair to expect them to act as though they had a degree of independence of their employment which they do not have. But this lack of independence in turn inevitably means that the task of a Department can never be other than secondary to the career security of the individuals employed in it. It is perfectly obvious from the enquiry reports that there were many civil servants who knew that what was going on was wrong, but who could not speak out about it because the penalty for doing so in terms of their jobs is simply too great. This is the root cause of the poor performance of the Irish Civil Service as now revealed.

Incompatibility of 'task' and 'career'

Individual civil servants may of course be morally equal or even superior to other citizens. However, the reward/punishment system under which they work need have little relationship to whatever the output of their Department is supposed to be. Above all, it is not symmetrical: rewards for success by no means balance penalties for failure:

> Whereas failure for yesterday's entrepreneur simply meant the loss of money (someone else's) failure for the modern bureaucrat means the loss of part of his identity. A report of his failure goes on his file - his paper identity, a paper *alter ego* that follows him inescapably through life -and alters his identity unfavourably. Innovation is more risky for the bureaucrat than for the entrepreneur. Loss of identity is far more serious than loss of money, even one's own (Thompson 1969 p. 5).

The search for 'cover'

Consequently, searching for "cover" against being blamed in the event of failure becomes a rule of life for a civil servant every bit as much as the search for profit is the rule for individuals who personally invest in their own risky projects. The result is that

> Inevitably, therefore, bureaucrats become dependent on the organisation for status and function - in the extreme case, for everything that is worthwhile. If they do not become alienated, they become organisation men, loyal to the organisation that supports them, thereby strengthening the system of organisational authority. Deprived of intrinsic rewards related to work or the rewards of the growing esteem of

their professional peers, they become largely dependent upon the extrinsic rewards distributed by the hierarchy of authority, thereby greatly reinforcing that institution. Their dependence upon organisational programs and procedures for whatever function they acquire induces a conservative attitude with regard to these programs and procedures. They may even hypostatise them into "natural laws", losing sight of their purely instrumental significance (Thompson 1969 p. 21).

Promotion as the only reward

When the only serious reward lies in promotion to a higher level within the hierarchy, opportunities for this become all-important, but since promotions are decided primarily by absence of failure, it is those who are best at arranging for their "cover' who move up through the hierarchy at the expense of those who take the actual task of the Department more seriously:

> Any form of organisation, including bureaus, will differentially reward those whose capabilities and attitudes best serve the organisation, and people will sort themselves out among forms of organisation depending upon their perceived reward. Bureaus reward a different type of personal behaviour from other forms, and, as a group, bureaucrats will be individuals who are most adept at this type of behaviour (Niskanen 1973 p. 12).

Obviously, outsiders have no right to blame a civil servant for behaving in this way - it is the only rational way to act, given the prevailing reward/punishment structure.

The threat of mediocrity

Unfortunately, as time passes, selection for promotion of the most career-focussed individuals tightens a bureaucratic organisation's hierarchical structure, and renders it progressively more self-regarding and less capable of delivering any outputs expected of it. From first-hand experience in Eastern Europe, Matejko has written a powerful description of this process:

> Functioning of the hierarchy and its survival becomes the primary goal and the original goals become only a window-dressing arrangement. There are several internal and external factors which contribute to such developments. One of them is the organisational hierarchy in itself which is so important in the daily existence of the people working for a given complex organisation that it soon occupies most of their attention.

> In order to preserve its internal balance, the hierarchical organisation depends on the loyalty of its functionaries; and the fact that such complex organisation is oriented towards longitudinal survival as a social institution has importance here. The "loyalists" win in the long run against the task-oriented innovators because the stability of the hierarchical organisation depends on them. Risky endeavours become gradually eliminated; everything within the organisation becomes stand-

ardised in order to limit the uncertainty. However, this progressing standardisation leads at the same time to the dominance of mediocrity. The cause of innovators and organisational nonconformists becomes hopelessly subordinated to the cause of mediocrities who provide the bulwark of the status quo. In the long run, the outcome is easy to predict: complex organisations run by mediocrities become mediocre in themselves; there is a growing cleavage between them and the changing environment (1986 p. 256).

The crucial point in Matejko's observation is that those who are focussed on their career path simply have to win in the long run against those who are more concerned with the task of their Department.

Political masters

A further difficulty is that a public bureaucracy's task is also partly what its political masters want it to be. Even an honest Minister will see it primarily in electoral terms, which can be how it contributes to his party's image, but even more, how it will affect financial contributions to its funds or how he can reward supporters with sinecures in semi-state bodies. A corrupt one will of course distort its task fundamentally in his own interest. Since job security and career progression within the civil service are everything to people whose skills have little value outside it, any Ministers who make it clear that they will use their power against the career of anyone who stands up to them, will in fact meet no resistance at all, because the cost to individuals is too great.

It is true that the Head of a Department has countervailing power, explicitly granted to him since the Ministers and Secretaries Act of 1924. Unfortunately, however, since by definition those who do reach the top have been the most successful at career progression, they are likely to have been correspondingly less concerned with their Department's task. The result is that by the time they achieve this power they have long since lost any desire to use it to confront a Minister. Similarly, at the Assistant Secretary level and even to some extent at that of Principal Officer, career-minded civil servants will have become particularly sensitive to the wishes, implicit as well as explicit, of their political masters, since it is these who control access to the final rungs of the ladder. Some tribunal evidence from senior civil servants suggested that they had lost (or perhaps never even had?) any vision at all of their Department's objective task.

What can be done about it?

Since the problem is that the cost to individual civil servants of doing their duty to their Department's task is so unacceptably high, the solution can only be some way of providing them with a degree of independence of their jobs. It is not to be expected that all civil servants will want this. Most are likely to prefer the line of least resistance, especially since this will do least damage to their promotion prospects. But the minority (probably the very small minority) who would act in the public interest if they could, are the necessary leaven in the entire system and the ones who must be supported. The most promising candidate for such support is practical endorsement of whistleblowing, the activity of bringing failure and wrongdoing to public notice.

Whistleblowing

The need to protect individuals who do this has been obvious in the private sector for many years. The great preponderance of the evidence about whistleblowers is that the organizations they challenge succeed in wrecking, not just their careers, but their lives, as has been illustrated in well-documented cases, such as those related to Hoffmann-LaRoche, Baring's Bank, British Biotech, and the U.S. tobacco firms. The whistleblower who does not suffer grievously for his actions is indeed a rare being.

Van Buitenen

The best known contemporary whistleblower, Paul van Buitenen, is doubly interesting, both in being from the public sector, and in having caused the resignation of the entire Jacques Santer European Commission. The importance of 'cover' to civil servants and the persisting damage to their careers of any errors on their records, means that a significant proportion of the energy in any bureaucracy is devoted to pretending that errors have not happened. This explains the intensity of the venom with which a bureaucracy turns on an individual who threatens to destroy this pretence. Apart from threats to van Buitenen that he would surely lose his job, and his actual suspension from it, his telephone was tapped and his computer access restricted, and before he presented the incriminating files to the Court of Auditors in Luxembourg he had to go into hiding for fear that he might be robbed of them. Fear of the consequences is therefore a most powerful deterrent to whistleblowing, and indeed van Buitenen is on record that if he had known what it would cost him and his family, he would never have begun his campaign.

His book does not just recount what happened, but also contains some valuable reflections on how a modern bureaucracy can be made more like one of the 'old' European ones:

> Whistleblowing is not a crime. It ought to be thought of as an important part of a modern and open administrative culture. Open and transparent organisations have nothing to fear from a whistleblower. Whistleblowing is not a 'necessary evil.' It is

a guarantee against the persistence of structurally endemic fraud and irregularities. It is an illusion to think that stricter regulations and a perfect audit policy can wipe out all major irregularities. In my own practice as assistant auditor in the Commission, but also before I worked in Brussels, I have observed on many occasions that major breakthroughs in ongoing investigations could only be achieved with the assistance of responsible whistleblowing.

The independent experts confirmed that the events leading up to the resignation of the former Commission demonstrated the value of officials whose conscience persuades them of the need to expose wrongdoings encountered in the course of their everyday duties. They also showed up how the reaction of superiors failed to live up to their legitimate expectations. Instead of offering ethical guidance, the hierarchy put additional pressure upon me (2000 p. 249).

Protective legislation

The results of legislation to deal with these problems have not so far been very encouraging (see Feldman 1999). In the U.S., the Civil Service Reform Act of 1978 was a failure, and was replaced by the 1989 Whistleblower Protection Act which was little better. The U.K. passed a Public Interest Disclosure Act in 1998 and in Ireland the similar Rabbitte Bill has all-party support in the Dail and is proceeding slowly towards becoming law.

The first case brought under the British legislation has recently been won, and the damages awarded were nearly £300,000. Whether this is adequate payment for losing a job will depend upon the whistleblower's future employment prospects, but if these have been damaged, such a sum would be poor compensation. Certainly, it would not be of much help to an Irish civil servant.

Release from secrecy obligation?

Every public bureaucracy extracts an undertaking from its members that they will keep all its affairs in strict secrecy. This adds a further strong element of deterrence to whistleblowing, since the more conscientious a civil servant is, the more reluctant he or she will be to break an undertaking which had been entered into freely. Van Buitenen's actions were sustained by his religious faith, and one of the most touching aspects of his account is how much anguish he suffered from this particular element of what he believed he had to do.

Yet, it is through this very secrecy undertaking that a practical way of providing some independence of their jobs to civil servants can be envisaged. An external, Ombudsman-type body could be given power to release any civil servant from this obligation, upon showing of good cause. This might not go as far as permitting public disclosure in the first instance, but might only allow information to be passed to some appropriate individual or body outside the bureaucracy. In van Buitenen's case, for example, his evidence that he could get no action from his own Directorate-General on the information he had collected, might have resulted in his being given explicit permission to disclose it to the Court of Auditors of the EU.

The very existence of such an external, independent body would instantly change the balance of power within a bureaucracy as between the whistleblower and his superiors who wish to cover up whatever he has discovered. At present, any such superior has enormous power of intimidation. But if a superior is deprived of this power, he has little choice except to act on an internal complaint, since otherwise he himself may be blamed both for causing an external supervisory body, or at the limit, even the public to learn about the wrongdoing or failure to perform to an acceptable standard.

Career damage

It has to be accepted as likely that a civil servant who is known even to have asked for release from his obligation to secrecy, even if he never has to use any freedom he may be granted, will be marked out as a troublemaker and that his career will suffer accordingly. It is certainly unrealistic to think that one who actually takes the step of bringing failures in his Department to public notice will ever have the career progress he might have expected if he had kept quiet about them. Even van Buitenen, who 'won' his battle with the European Commission (at least to the extent that the Santer Commission lost) has completely failed to get back into any aspect of the audit function for which he is trained and in which he is so obviously effective. He has also had to agree not to accept invitations to speak. All this is in spite of the extent to which his 'rehabilitation' is being watched carefully by a wide public, and of the decoration bestowed on him by the Queen of the Netherlands.

Option to retire?

A possibility well worth exploring as a means of dealing with this is extension of a provision which already exists in Germany. In the two highest ranks of the Civil Service there, an official can be transferred by his Minister without any reason being given, but if the change is not acceptable, the official can retire on full pay (Plowden 1994 p. 95). Why should a similar provision not apply to all ranks if subsequent discrimination against an official because of whistleblowing through loyalty to his Department's task could be shown?

If this could not be contemplated, it should still be possible to rely on the pensionable nature of civil service jobs. The external, Ombudsman-type body which had earlier given the whistleblower release from his undertaking of secrecy could also be given the power to award him an option to retire on pension, if his career has suffered as a result of using this freedom. Such a body should also be able to apply some factor to increase his pension at the date of retirement, to take account of the fact that pensions are usually calculated as a proportion of final salary, and the whistleblower is virtually sure to have forfeited a career path that would lead to a high one.

Giving the external body this additional power would undermine the position of those who wish to cover up wrongdoing still further. They would then run the risk, not just of being blamed because their inaction resulted in the wrongdoing being revealed to an external supervisory body or even to the public, but also for the extra pension costs (and adverse publicity) which will have to be borne. If the external body could give some sort of undertaking on the pension issue on the basis of evidence presented to it in confidence by the whistleblower before he makes use of his release from his obligation of secrecy, it would be all the more effective in preventing covering-up and inaction within bureaucracies, before problems reach the stage where public revelation is the only way of dealing with them. If proper action had been taken about van Buitenen's discoveries when it should have been, M. Santer would still be President of the European Commission, even if without Mme. Cresson as a fellow-Commissioner.

Transparency is not enough

There is another way in which such an external body with the power suggested could be beneficial to public bureaucracies. Van Buitenen places his faith in 'transparency' as a cure for bureaucratic corruption, and some countries are attempting to improve their Civil Services through this means. However, not everything can be opened to public gaze, and transparency has its own disadvantage. There is growing evidence that in countries where Freedom of Information Acts have been introduced, civil servants are recording less of what they do. In Ireland, for example, top Civil Servants are known to have destroyed their diaries, lest an enquiry under the Freedom of Information Act might reveal their involvement in decisions. This is to be expected, in light of the bureaucratic practice, referred to earlier, of searching for 'cover' against attribution of blame. But a bureaucratic organisation is only able to operate to the extent that it has more or less complete information, an important aspect of which is that it is codified, indexed and accessible. This reflects the record-keeping activity which civil servants have always been derided for worshipping. To the extent, therefore, that records are being replaced by informal communication - or worse, by informal decision-making - bureaucracies are moving still further away from the standards of the 'old' bureaucracies that were so effective.

The external body proposed above would preserve whatever secrets need to be kept in the public interest in all but the rarest cases. As well as this, its existence should bring about a great improvement in the morale of civil servants. At the present time, it must be extremely frustrating for the best of them to be aware of incompetence and even wrongdoing and to feel helpless to do anything about it, because the personal cost of taking action is so terribly high. By providing them with a degree of independence of their jobs, albeit only in crisis situations, the proposed arrangements seem to hold out considerable promise of ability to change the operating standards of the civil service for the better.

References

Feldman, Estelle, 1999: 'Whistleblower protection: comparative legal developments.' *Irish Law Times* 17, 264-72.

Kingston, William, 1983: 'Ideas, Civil Servants and Keynes,' *Economic Affairs*, February.

Matejko, Alexander J., 1986: *The Self-Defeating Organization*. New York, Praeger Publishers.

Niskanen, William A., 1973: *Bureaucracy: Servant or Master?* London, Institute of Economic Affairs.

Plowden, William, 1994: *Ministers and Mandarins*. London, Institute for Public Policy Research.

Schumpeter, Joseph A., [1942] 1958: *Capitalism, Socialism and Democracy*. New York, Harper and Row.

Thompson, Victor A., *Bureaucracy and Innovation*. Alabama, University of Alabama Press.

van Buitenen, Paul, 2000: *Blowing the Whistle*. London, Politicos.

Chapter VII

'Systemic Corporate Failure of Public Administration:' Reflections on the Travers Report
(First published 2005)

Introduction

An earlier article[1] (Chapter VI) called attention to how enquiries set up primarily into the doings of politicians, showed up appalling levels of contributory incompetence and worse on the part of the public service. Its diagnosis was that the actual task of their departments can never be the primary interest of public servants, and that the few who might act as a leaven no longer have the degree of independence they need for it; the prescription for a partial cure was formal arrangements for going public about wrongdoing—'whistleblowing'—so that these few individuals could deal with evident and serious problems without having to sacrifice their careers. The very existence of such arrangements, it was claimed, would be such a strong deterrent that they would need to be used only very rarely.

Since that article was published, further evidence which supports its diagnosis has appeared in a series of investigations of public service failures. Of these, the Morris Tribunal reports on police criminality in Donegal have been the most shocking[2]. The performance of the Department of Justice in monitoring the inability of Garda management to deal with it has yet to be probed, but we already know enough to recognise how prescient was the comment of Professor Dermot Walsh, some years ago, that 'the price paid for this sacred cow of police independence is a major black hole in the democratic accountability of the police'[3].

The Comptroller and Auditor-General has continued to detail how an entire series of Government departments and bodies, such as the National Roads Authority, seem to be totally unable to control massive public expenditures. Not a single Government department awoke in time to the vast potential for property developers to misuse a law intended only to allow homeowners to buy out their ground rents, even though the possibility had been raised twice by the Law Reform Commission. In comparison with the grave issues and the enormous amounts of

---

[1] William Kingston (2001): 'What Can We Do About the Civil Service?' *Studies* 90 (359) 320-330.

[2] Morris Tribunal. Available at: www.morristribunal.ie/images/sitecontent_80.pdf

[3] Dermot Walsh (1999): 'Who Guards the Guards?' *Studies* 88 (350) 154-163.

money at stake in these and similar cases, the ability of another State-run institution, the Abbey Theatre, to lose well over a million Euro without anyone there adverting to it, seems hardly worth mentioning.

However, we have learned most about how the civil service operates from the enquiry by John Travers into the Health Department's performance in charging poor people for long-stay institutional care[4]. What it reveals is more damning than even the findings of the Cromien report on the Department of Justice had been[5]. The illegality of the Department of Health's behaviour over nearly three decades will now cost the State many hundreds of millions of Euro. Travers's summing up, 'long-term overall systemic corporate failure of public administration' at the highest levels, certainly has very much wider application than just to the Department of Health and Children.

The Travers Report

What Travers had to report on had begun with a Ministerial Regulation, expressed in a departmental circular to the Health Boards (No. 7 of 1976) advising them how to charge medical card holders for maintenance in institutions. This was in the face of the Department's own legal advisor's view (sustained, to his or her credit, over many following years) that in light of a decision by the Supreme Court (the McInerney case)[6] this could not be done without a change in the law. In 1978, the Department was told of Counsel's Opinion obtained by the Eastern Health Board to the same effect. In the same year, the Registrar of the Office of the Wards of Court queried circular 7/76 and suggested that the Department should challenge him in the Courts to get clarification, but the Department would not do this.

Even more revealing, although there were not many individual challenges to the circular at the outset, because of 'the physical and/or mental vulnerability of the people concerned,' when some medical card holders did refuse to pay the charges, the Department advised the Health Boards not to sue them, because of the virtual certainty of losing the case. The Ombudsman specifically raised the issue of this illegality in five of his Annual Reports, 'very explicitly' in oral presentation to the Oireachtas joint Committee on Health and Children in 2001. The following year (presumably because more people were refusing to pay the charges) the South Eastern Health Board sought Counsel's Opinion on the issue

---

[4] John Travers: 'Report on Certain Issues of Management and Administration in the Department of Health and Children Associated with the Practice of Charges for Persons in Long-Stay Institutions and Related Matters.' Available at: www.oireachtas.ie/viewdoc.asp?fn=/documents/Committees29thDail/CommitteeReports2005/document3.pdf

[5] See Estelle Feldman (1999) 'Accountability: a Case Study' *Studies* 88 (350) 141-153.

[6] *In re Maud McInerney*, a Ward of Court [1976-7] ILRM 229.

and this too was unequivocal about the illegality of the practice. A Report of the Human Rights Commission in April 2003 also could not have been clearer to the same effect.

Over all these years, as Travers notes, an immense amount of administrative resources within the Department of Health were wasted 'in attempting to defend a legally suspect charging regime and in undertaking a sequence of reviews of a practice clearly seen to be problematic.' An internal review in 1982 acknowledged that the practices in question were illegal, but nothing was done about it; in 1987, a Memorandum was brought to the Government which could have dealt with the matter, but it got no further, and in 1992, another internal review came to the same conclusion as that ten years earlier, again without any follow-through.

Stimulated by the import of the South-Eastern Health Board's Counsel's Opinion, in December 2003 the Department's Management Advisory Committee at last decided to set up a working group in preparation for getting a definitive ruling from the Attorney-General. A month later this group sent to the Department's Secretary-General a draft of the request for this, for his signature. The letter was never sent, no one can explain why, but the minutes of the Committee's meeting in March 2004 wrongly recorded that it had been. CEOs of the Health Boards were also wrongly told in October that 'legal options were being considered.' Finally, after a question in the Dáil, the Minister herself discovered the failure and insisted that the Attorney General's view should be obtained. Within a month, he had ruled definitively that the Department's practice was wrong, and had been wrong for 28 years.

A Bill was then drafted which included a provision to make the charges legal retrospectively. Not surprisingly, when it was passed by the Oireachtas, the President sent it to the Supreme Court, where this provision was ruled to be unconstitutional, on the basis of the property rights clause in the Constitution, not because it was retrospective. The briefing Paper which had been provided to the Minister for her speech introducing this Bill did not mention the working group of December, 2003, nor the letter to the Attorney-General which that group had drafted for the Secretary-General to sign, nor the minutes of the meeting which wrongly recorded that it had been sent, nor the fact that it was never sent at all. It was economy with the truth on the grand scale. When the Minister discovered this, she appointed John Travers to investigate how the Department could have got things so wrong for so long. But by the time he got involved, as if in a final show of incompetence or breach of trust, a crucial file had disappeared. Incredibly, he found that one of his recommendations had to be that the Department should 'put in place an effective system for logging the movement of files'.

Frustrating the Ombudsman

The performance of the Department of Health and Children is put into a wider context by the comments of the Ombudsman on the Travers Report to the relevant Oireachtas Committee in June 2005[7]. She claimed that nothing of what Travers had uncovered had been revealed to her predecessor. If it had been, she insisted, it 'would have established, in the language of Section 4 of the Ombudsman Act, 1980, that the Department's actions (and those of the health boards in reliance on the Department's position) were being 'taken without proper authority'. She added that he would have reported it to the Committee, and,

> Furthermore, in dealing with complaints in this area, it is very likely that the Ombudsman would have completed investigations and made recommendations providing for appropriate redress. However, in a situation where he did not know of this evidence, and in spite of the strength of the argument he was himself making, the Ombudsman stopped short of making recommendations in individual cases.

In his presentation to the Dáil Committee in 2001, her predecessor had referred to 'a breakdown in the accountability relationship between Ministers and senior civil servants and at the very least a distinct lack of transparency in that relationship.' What the Travers Report has revealed is in fact even worse. The Office of the Ombudsman has been established as an independent organ of the State, specifically to protect citizens from misuse of power by the executive branch. Not alone did the Department of Health misuse its power over poor people; it *actively obstructed* the Ombudsman in doing his statutory duty to protect them.

In the present case, therefore, we have a government Department, as a matter of deliberate and sustained policy, frustrating the intentions of the Oireachtas in passing the law which set up the Ombudsman's Office. This even went so far, the present Ombudsman told the Committee, that in intensive discussions, 'the Department purported to have been unaware of the Supreme Court decision in the McInerney case.' This is neither inadvertence, nor confusion about the legal situation, but straightforward corrupt institutional behaviour, caused because over 28 years no senior person in the Department cared about what it was supposed to be doing. It is acting in relation to the body politic in just the same way as cancer does in a physical body.

Can anything be done?

An unusual and welcome feature of the Travers Report is that in it he raises questions about 'the balance of morality,' possibly because of the vulnerability of

---

[7] See Submission by the Ombudsman to the Oireachtas Joint Committee on Health and Children, 3 June 2005. Available at: www.ombudsman.gov.ie/24e6_156.htm

those who suffered from the Health Department's illegal behaviour. There are two aspects to this. Firstly, the Department maintained to the end that they had always acted 'in good faith,' even though there was not one single bit of legal support for their position and a mass of legal expertise against it. Ignorance and stupidity they might get away with, but 'good faith' is an insult to intelligence. It is bureaucrat-speak for 'we didn't advert to what we were doing, because we didn't care.' Secondly, there was something particularly despicable about a policy which included advising the Health Boards not to pursue those who refused to pay the charges, because they would lose in Court. As the Minister herself later put it to a joint Oireachtas Committee, this meant that those who could afford legal advice did not have to pay, but the poorest did. Travers also asks:

> What if the corporate entity does not take appropriate steps to deal with the uncertainties that exist? What can, or should, individual officials within the corporate entity do in such a situation? Indeed, what should officials external to the corporate entity but working elsewhere in the public service do if they become aware of serious legal uncertainties surrounding particular actions or practices?

As the public service is structured at present, there is nothing that an individual can do, or can be expected to do. The price of taking any action which could be effective, in terms of that individual's career path, is too high, and it is this career path, not the task of his or her Department, that is the primary concern of any public servant. This is why there is need for an independent Commission, which could be approached by an individual with a request to be released from his or her undertaking to keep Service matters secret. The same Commission would also have power to award compensation to such a person for any resulting adverse career effects. If this had been in force at any time during the 28 years covered by the Travers Report, it would only have needed a single civil servant who took the responsibilities of his or her Department seriously to save the country many millions of Euro.

In any group of public servants, many will have been so formed by the system that they will mindlessly endorse established policies, just because they *are* established. Typical of these would be whoever concealed information from the Ombudsman, even to the extent of claiming that the Department was unaware of the McInerney case. Others will evaluate policies and performance solely in terms of their effect on their own careers. Unfortunately, these are the ones who tend to get promoted, but promotion does not increase their concern for their Department's task. The Irish system, inherited from the British one, leaves a considerable power in the hands of a Departmental Secretary for a formal Minute recording disagreement with his political master. Unfortunately, by the time this power is achieved, only the rarest of the individuals concerned will have kept alive any desire they might ever have had to use it. In the present case, such a Minute could clearly have dealt with the apparent reluctance of the Government which came into power in March 1987, to revive its predecessor's draft Bill to regularise the charging situation.

The majority of civil servants will keep their heads down, like those at the November 2004 meeting of the Management Advisory Committee of the Department of Health when the clearly incorrect minutes of the March meeting came up again. Travers notes about this meeting that nobody 'who would have known the correct position, appears to have intervened to put matters straight.' But we could hope that there would also be a few for whom their Department's task is important, and who would take action towards its achievement if they could. These are the crucial few who need to be provided with some way of going public on an issue without fear of damaging their livelihood.

'It seems to me,' the Ombudsman told the Oireachtas Committee in June 2005, 'that in the aftermath of the Travers Report, the nature of the relationship between the executive, between Ministers and senior civil servants, requires urgent attention. On the wider issue is that the model of government, meant to underpin and support the workings of government, is no longer fully relevant.' This is precisely part of the argument of the earlier article. An aspect of the model that is no longer relevant is that of the old, class-based European civil services, whose senior members had been educated in a particular code of values and who had a significant degree of independence of politicians. Their replacement by people without those values, and who have no comparable independence, of character as much as in the financial sense, is all too apparent from the Travers report.

The other side of the coin of lack of independence is relief from individual responsibility. It is the diffusion of responsibility for decisions within the public service which explains why so many government projects involving the use of consultants have been such mind-boggling failures. The latest of these (also in the Department of Health) is that computerisation budgeted at €8 million has had to be abandoned after costing €160 million, with a new budget of €250 million for its completion. Much of this has been spent on consultants, but consultants can only be as effective as the management to which they are working, and no Committee (the standard civil service way of avoiding individual responsibility) can manage well. When building up General Electric (UK) Arnold Weinstock had a rule that no consultant could be engaged anywhere throughout that huge organization without his personal approval, because private sector managers are selected, promoted and paid to take individual responsibility. Failure to grasp this simple principle has led the civil service into the mistaken belief that it can make up for its lack of specific expertise by hiring consultants. It cannot, because it is intrinsically incapable of using them effectively.

'Whistleblowing'

'Whistleblowing' is an unhappy word for the activity which needs supporting arrangements, because it carries connotations of a 'sneaks' charter' or of cranks being let loose upon well-functioning organizations. However, it is the only word we have at present. The most active centre for spreading information about it is Public Concern at Work in London, which owes its origin, like many other enlightened initiatives, to the Joseph Rowntree Foundation[8]. Allied Irish Banks, for example, has recognized how many of its own past troubles could have been avoided if even a single individual had felt able to go public about a serious emerging problem. Consequently, it has put a scheme in place whereby any employee who is concerned about wrongdoing in the Bank can approach either the Chief Executive or the Chairman directly. It is naive to think that this in itself will produce any worthwhile results, but it has been supplemented by a provision for approaching Public Concern at Work, and it is only realistic to believe that it is to this latter body any future complaints are likely to be made[9].

Given the amount of money which the Government will now have to reimburse to people who were charged illegally, if any individual or group in the Department of Health had felt able to take a stand on the issue, at almost any time over the 28 years it existed, virtually any multiple of their salaries as compensation for the inevitable destruction of their careers would still have left the country a huge nett gainer. Any proposal to introduce such a scheme would have to begin by proper understanding that it could only be effective if it provides whistleblowers with a level of financial protection which goes far beyond anything contemplated at present.

The highest award so far made in Britain under the 1999 Public Interest Disclosure Act is the equivalent of about €750,000. When weighted by the chances of not getting such an amount, this would be poor compensation for any well-paid individual (such as a member of the Management Advisory Committee of the Department of Health and Children). Such a person would have to face certain loss of promotion prospects and probably some version of the treatment recently devised by the Human Resources Department of Aer Lingus for obtaining 'voluntary' redundancies. No matter how much good in the abstract a whistleblower

[8] Website: www.pcaw.co.uk
[9] Allied Irish Banks: Annual Report, 2004.

may do, the record shows that he or she pays the price of being made virtually unemployable. A typical illustration of this is that a Committee of the City of London, investigating the collapse of Baring's Bank, claimed that a compliance officer whose persistent worries had not been listened to by the Board, had not done enough; they said that he should have resigned his job to get attention. Yet this Committee was representative of the very people who would have ensured that if he had in fact done this, he would never work in the City again.

The main benefit of arrangements for whistleblowing is that it is such a powerful deterrent to the besetting sin of all bureaucracies: the cover-up. Within the civil service, it would consequently take very few cases to improve performance dramatically. At present, the danger of attribution of responsibility for failure, and of a penalty for covering up failure, is very low. If the risk of revelation of wrongdoing of whatever kind were to be increased by more transparency as proposed, better behaviour would be bound to follow. In the Health charges case, for example, it is possible to hope that over nearly three decades, those in charge would have done the right thing, not because they wanted to, but in fear lest some individual who was protected in this way might shout 'Stop!'

In spite of all the potential advantages of such arrangements, it does not seem likely that the Government will take any effective action in this direction. Pat Rabbitte introduced a whistleblowing Bill in the last Dáil, which had all-party support. This fell with that Dáil, and the Government has now turned its back on it, claiming (without any apparent rationale) that 'the provision of statutory protection on a sectoral basis would provide a better and more focused approach to dealing with the issue'[10]. In any event, the Rabbitte Bill only dealt with the private sector, whereas the public sector has at least equally urgent need for an arrangement of this kind.

Conclusion

As a product of the Irish public service himself, Travers's report is not short of *pietas*, forcing him to make expected genuflections to 'long and proud tradition of public administration,' 'high standards,' 'professionalism and integrity,' 'compares favourably with most other countries,' and so on. However, the facts he had to record in it simply cannot be reconciled with such claims. Instead, they confirm once again how in every bureaucracy 'functioning of the hierarchy and its survival becomes the primary goal and the original goals become only a win-

---

[10] Reply to parliamentary question by Minister of State at the Department of Enterprise, Trade and Employment (Mr. Killeen) 16 November 2004.

dow-dressing arrangement[11]. The inability of the Health branch of the Association of Higher Civil Servants, in the face of the overwhelming evidence, to accept Travers's conclusion of 'long-term systemic failure of administration' shows how far the Irish bureaucracy is irreformable in itself[12].

So is his Report only one more study that will be filed away and ignored? Perhaps not, because, apart from its inherent thoroughness and quality, it could be a focus for the growing body of evidence that the '[Irish] model of government is no longer fully relevant,' as the Ombudsman put it. Sooner or later, the search for a better model, of which an essential component would be a significantly changed civil service, will have to begin. For that beginning, there is much to be gained from close study of the contents of the can of worms that Travers has opened.

Winston Churchill endorsed the view that democracy is the worst form of government, except all those other forms that have been tried from time to time[13]. Democracy's fundamental requirement is respect for the rule of law, in contrast to the contempt for it that the civil service culture of the Department of Health showed for so long until the political system (in spite of all the attempts there have been to try to shift the blame) finally caught up with it. There cannot be democracy without public administration, but the more we in Ireland learn about how this actually operates, the gloomier the picture of this appears. However, there is one consolation, which is by no means unimportant: we could live in a country where there were no revealing investigations such as that of Travers, so that we could never know just how bad things are.

---

[11] Alexander I. Matejko (1986) *The Self-Defeating Organization*, 256. New York, Praeger Publishers.
[12] In their submission to the Oireachtas Joint Committee, available at: www.debates.oireachtas. ie/Debate.aspx?F=HEJ20050609.xml&Node=H2&Page=5
[13] Hansard, 11 November 1947, col. 206.

Chapter VIII
An Alternative Agenda for Public Service Reform
(First published 2004)

In recent articles in *Studies* (2001) and the *Political Quarterly* (2002) I called attention to how enquiries set up primarily to enquire into the doings of politicians in Ireland and Britain, have shown up numerous cases where evil could have been stopped in its tracks if even a single public employee who knew what was going on, had threatened to go public about it. Irish transfusions of lethal blood are an obvious example. My diagnosis was that the actual task of their departments can never be the primary interest of public servants, and that the few who might act as a leaven no longer have the degree of independence they need for it; my prescription was formal arrangements for whistleblowing, so that individuals could deal with wrong-doing without having to sacrifice their careers. I argued that the very existence of such arrangements would be such a strong deterrent to the besetting sin of all bureaucracies, the cover-up, that they would need to be used only very rarely.

This topic deserves to be put into a wider context, which means examining the laws, especially the laws relating to property, within which public servants have to work. With increasing frequency, these laws are so poorly matched to their objectives that it is simply impossible to administer them well. This in turn results from excessive concentration by policy-makers on intervention rather than on shaping the legal structure. Two Irish cases illustrate very well the general principle that if we do not get the laws right, intervention will not work, but to the extent that we do get them right, it is unnecessary. The first of these comes from the Report of the Ombudsman for 2001, and the second from that of the Comptroller and Auditor-General for 2002.

Planning 'crisis'

The Ombudsman stressed that the country's entire Planning system is 'in crisis' because the authorities lack resources to police conformity with permissions.

The implication is that this crisis can only be dealt with by multiplying the number of employees in Planning Offices around the country. This is the classic bureaucratic response: when something is found to be wrong, going to the root of a problem will affect vested interests, some of which may be perceived be able to affect senior public servants' career paths through political influence.

The standard way of avoiding this is to institute or expand some form of regulatory regime, which also has the advantage of generating more opportunities for promotion. Not surprisingly, world-wide evidence is that such arrangements fall under the control of the interests they are meant to discipline – the process is called 'regulatory capture.'

In reality, the planning problem is one which could be solved without the need to recruit a single extra employee, by nothing more a one-line amendment to the law, analogous to the law which imposes stamp duty on many kinds of contracts. This is a tax which no-one ever attempts to evade, and yet it costs nothing whatever to police, for the simple reason that the Courts will almost never consider a document which should have been properly stamped but which has not been. In order to avoid having only a piece of paper which purports to be a contract, but which is legally worthless, therefore, holders themselves and their solicitors take good care to see that documents are stamped.

If a building contract which was not in exact compliance in every particular with planning permission was made similarly unenforceable, the policing of permissions would be done by builders, with no cost to the State, and at the same time more meticulously than by any Planning inspector. Moreover, the authorities would no longer have 'retentions' to deal with. These are cases where buildings are actually erected without permission, or in defiance of a permission, and they almost always involve political pressure being brought to bear on the planners. As a result, they have been the vehicle for some of the worst breaches of planning policies.

Any legislation for this would have to ensure that 'Contract' meant an agreement between a developer (i.e. the holder of the planning permission) and an architect, as well as with a builder. Moreover, even though there are not many developers who are their own builders, it is particularly easy for such people to flout planning regulations. Consequently, in such cases, every contract in relation to a building project would have to be unenforceable if it is for work that is outside the planning permission.

That is, if both developer and builder were the same entity, a sub-contractor responsible for only part of the work, e.g. plastering or electrical installation, would have to make sure that what they were doing was in accordance with the permission which had been granted, if they were to have an enforceable contract. Of course, in the majority of cases there is a single main contractor. This contractor and the architect would then take responsibility for compliance, if they wanted to be sure of getting paid, and sub-contractors would not have to concern themselves with the details of the planning permission.

One of the most notorious retention cases was that of the Central Bank building in Dame St. The architects deliberately designed this thirty feet higher than its planning permission, no doubt expecting that retention would be granted once the work had already been done. At the time, the planners said they had too few staff even to be aware of what was happening until the roof was almost completed. Retention was in fact granted for the building in an incomplete state, which is why the exposed internal structure at the top was a feature of the Dublin architectural scene for several decades.

If the suggested amendment to the law had been in force then, it is quite unimaginable that the builders would have signed the contract to build according to the architects' specification, when the fact that this flouted the planning permission meant that this contract would not be enforceable through the Courts. The Bank could not possibly have been built otherwise than in exact accordance with the approval it had been given by the Planners.

The C&AG and the Revenue Commissioners

The Comptroller and Auditor-General's Report reveals the case of a developer who 'came into the tax system by taking advantage of the tax amnesty of 1988,' by paying only the equivalent of €79,000 for 17 years' activities.

The Revenue authorities did not think that this was enough, but failed to press the matter. He went on to carry out developments during the 1990s which were 'valued at over €125 million ,' operating through at least 35 companies, each in a different tax district. In total, these paid only €250,000 in corporation tax over the entire period, during which they received net *refunds* of €6 million in Value-Added-Tax. When the developer sold his house for €3.9 million at a time when residential property tax was in force, he was absolved from paying it 'because his declared income was below the income threshold.' Of one of his shell firms where €442,000 of tax had to be written off as uncollectable, the Comptroller noted that the Revenue Commissioners' staff had not adverted to any connection between it and 'the individual, the amnesty payment or his other companies.'

Inevitably, attention has focused on the managerial incompetence which allowed the insulation from one another of all the tax districts and the amnesty, income tax, corporation tax, VAT and residential property tax divisions. But, as the Comptroller points out, this case also raises the issue of the law of limited liability Companies. Laws, like people, are subject to corruption, and laws relating to property rights like this one, are especially vulnerable. As John Stuart Mill wrote, 'the laws of property have never yet conformed to the principles on which the institution of private property rests' ([1862, Book II Ch. I). It is certainly the

case that modern Corporation law has been twisted in ways that leave it far away
from the inspiration of its origins.

Limited liability

General incorporation with limited liability is a social innovation of incalcu-
lable value in facilitating investment, and so bringing about economic development. In this part of the world, it goes back to the 1856 Act, whose usefulness was
seen to be so great that it was copied throughout Europe within ten years.

Before this, limitation of liability to the amount of one's investment in a project could only be obtained in companies which had a Royal Charter or in respect
of which an individual Act of Parliament was passed, such as for the building of
canals and railways. Apart from these, co-operative investment had to be made
through some form of partnership, sometimes set up as non-incorporated joint
stock companies. This has the great disadvantage that each partner is liable for all
the partnership's debts right up to the limit of his or her fortune (as many members of Lloyds insurance syndicates recently experienced to their great cost).

Limiting liability to the amount of one's stake removes this huge risk from
investment, and also enables investors to spread their risks and separates ownership from management. In these ways, it has underwritten enormous world-wide
development of large-scale and professionally-managed industry. It is interesting
and relevant that some of the prosperity associated with the era of Grattan's parliament may have been due to the provision for *limited partnerships* for a 15 year
term which it introduced in 1782 (French, 1990). This way of investing did not
come to the United Kingdom until 1908.

Limited liability is therefore not in any sense a right, indeed a right which
business men take for granted. It is simply a *privilege* granted by Society for a
public purpose. There is no reason why Society should not require, as a condition
of granting this privilege, that the identity of anyone taking advantage of it should
be publicly known. No investor in any honest project could have any basis for
claiming that such a condition is in the slightest degree unreasonable, since they
can invest cooperatively through a partnership if they wish.

Unlimited secrecy

Secrecy forms no necessary part of the grant of the privilege of limited liability,
yet during the development of Company law, the power to have absolute secrecy
as to ownership has come to be included. Indeed, in many cases to-day, the *primary* objective in using a limited liability company for investment is to conceal
the identities of the true actor(s) in a business undertaking. For example, in the

case of the suspicious sale of the Johnston, Mooney and O'Brien site in Balls-bridge some years ago, the Government-appointed investigator had to admit a high degree of failure to identify the beneficial owners of the site after three years' trying to penetrate through a series of such shell companies. A typical difficulty encountered was that

> [T]he true ownership of Freezone by Mr. Desmond was effected through the mech-anism of allowing Mr. Probets to appear as the beneficial owner of the Company, even though the registered owners of the shares were two chartered accountants in the Isle of Man. Each of these executed a declaration that they held the is-sued shares as nominees for Mr. Probets, but from approximately the time that these declarations were executed, Mr. Desmond held the option from Mr. Probets, enabling him to acquire the shares of the Company for the nominal amount of £1 (Glackin 1993 Section 4.71).

And the cynicism with which business men use the privilege of limited li-ability coupled with secrecy which they have been granted by the State is also evident from the same investigation. When the Inspector asked about the identity of 'J. and N. McMahon,' who had paid £1.5 million into one of the companies, Mr. Desmond told him 'they were not real people. You pick out references that suit in the transfer of funds' (Glackin 1993 Section 8.4.4.).

Just as the sequence of companies in this case frustrated the Inspector, in the taxation case quoted earlier, the use of multiple companies, each in a different tax district, completely defeated the Revenue Commissioners.

'Non-justiciable' agreements

Yet here again, getting the law right by making a simple change in it, could provide, if not a complete solution, then a very significant one. In this case, the model is the Sherman Act of 1890 in the United States. This was the first legisla-tion against the 'Trusts,' the powerful groupings of firms in railways, steel and other industries which were sharing out markets between themselves against the public interest. Sherman simply made any agreement in restraint of trade *non-justiciable*, that is, unenforceable through the Courts. (This had also been the situation of unincorporated joint-stock companies in England between 1720 and 1825).

Just as easily as in the planning case, therefore, a one-line amendment to the relevant law could make any agreement in relation to a limited company non-jus-ticiable to the extent that it has the intention or effect of preventing the company's beneficial ownership from being known. The transfer of shares from the founding shareholders (usually two solicitors' clerks) to another party would be such a non-justiciable contract, because any pre-signing of blank and undated forms without identifying in whose interest this was being done, would have introduced a fatal flaw in it, through concealing the true situation from the public. So would secret holding of shares as nominees, as well as undisclosed options to buy shares. Investors would then have to choose between having limited liability or keeping their identities secret, because they could no longer have both, legally endorsed.

Of course, such a change in the law on its own could not deal with those cases where there is perfect trust between an owner and whoever he wants to front for him, but trust unsupported by legal sanctions is a week reed, and where large amounts of money are involved it could be expected to be very scarce indeed. Moreover, in so far as an investor is not working completely on his own, for example if a property developer needed substantial finance secured against a site, and the latter is held through a Company which conceals his or his associates' beneficial ownership, he would be unable to get it. No bank would put up money if the legal position was that neither an investor nor anyone fronting for him would be able to provide it with an enforceable lien on collateral.

Getting the laws right

If solving serious problems is as easy as this, why is so little attention paid to getting the laws right? The obvious answer is that this task is nobody's business. Politicians want to be seen to be *active*. Civil servants are trained to work on individual trees, and the habit of this is poor training for those who get to the top of the system, in looking after a wood – as the tax case so clearly shows. Vested interests, of course, do not want any change in arrangements which suit them, and these interests influence politicians. When the government sets up a group to give it advice, such as that on Company Law Reform, the need for it to be representative ensures that such interests – whose representatives are invariably far more highly motivated than civil servant members - will be able to prevent radical changes from being included the group's Report.

Consequently, nothing but good could come from introducing formal arrangements within the Civil Service for achieving public objectives by getting the laws right, instead of intervening in the economy. This would mean developing a small elite group in each Department whose *only* function would be to suggest how changed or new legislation could contribute, before any decision is taken about an approach to a particular problem. Such a group would provide specific alternatives to the measures of intervention which the mass of the Civil Service could be counted on to continue to favour.

If the institutional resistance to such a change could be overcome, it could be anticipated that the success of such 'law-devising' groups would open the way to further reforms of the civil service. At their best, these might be made to reflect the reality that under modern conditions, and also in countries other than Ireland, bureaucracy has an indispensable role to play, quite different from that envisaged by reformers who want it to be more like private enterprise, in the interest of 'efficiency.' This role is far more important than just to be the performer of whatever activities elected governments decide are to be carried on under their own control, and any reforms must ultimately be commensurate with this.

Property Rights, Democracy and Bureaucracy

To understand why, it is necessary to consider three themes which are usually discussed and researched separately, but which are interlinked because of a problem which all advanced countries face to-day. This arises because democracy is a property rights system, in which the vote is a right given to numbers simply as numbers, to counterbalance wealth resulting from other kinds of property. Without this balance, democracy either cannot begin (illustrated by the Soviet Union) or quickly ends up in despotism (illustrated in different degrees by ex-colonial countries). In Ireland, incidentally, the proportional representation electoral system tilts this balance towards numbers.

However, because voters' interests are diffused, and the interests of holders of other kinds of property rights tend to be concentrated, the latter have an inherent advantage, as discussed by Olson (1965). Since he wrote, the effects of mass media and the consequent escalating costs of getting elected have put politicians and voters even further into the power of wealth-owners (cf. Newman 1999). Coupled with this has been the fragmentation of bureaucracies into 'Agencies' in the United States, 'Ministries' or 'Departments' in Europe. So far from articulating the public good, these often have links to interest groups, which unfortunately are being greatly strengthened by the growth of public/private partnerships. Correspondingly, their activities are no longer contributing as they should to the democratic balance.

Questions like these indicate that the important issue is no longer that of the State versus private enterprise, in the way both socialists and their opponents have seen it to be for so long. It is now a question of freedom versus a 'patronage state' which has been significantly captured by private interests. In this, the machinery of government is increasingly operated by the civil service in the interest of property owners, mediated by politicians. But, as Schumpeter wrote of the State, 'It is part of its nature that it opposes individual egoism as a representative of a common purpose. Only then is it a separate, distinguishable social entity' ([1918] 1991, 110). To the extent that democratic government has been failing in this opposition, it is on the way towards fulfilling Marx's prophecy that it would become nothing more than 'the committee of the bourgeoisie.'

A new role for bureaucracy

This is why there is need for reinforcement of the 'vote' side of the balance from a third element, which is an independent bureaucracy. As Schumpeter also wrote, idealistically:-

> [D]emocratic government in modern industrial society must be able to command... the services of a well-trained bureaucracy of good standing and tradition, endowed with a strong sense of duty and a no less strong *esprit de corps* [which]... must also be strong enough to guide and, if need be, instruct the politicians who head the ministries. In order to be able to do this it must be in a position to evolve principles of its own and be sufficiently independent to assert them. It must be a power in its own right ([1943] 1950, 293).

Contemporary civil servants may lament the passing of an era (before the coming of 'special advisers') when this was at least partially true, but at its core is the important vision that somewhere in society there has to be some source where the public good is independently articulated. Voters are unable to do this for themselves in anything other than vague terms, whilst for property-owners it can reduce to some version of 'what's good for General Motors is good for the country.' Schumpeter clearly thought of the Civil Service as such a source, but Gawthrop has shown how existing arrangements force bureaucrats towards the self-serving pole of a continuum of interests and away from the 'public good' pole (1998, 134). The public good can only be articulated by those who are independent of interests, as far as this is possible.

Prussia and France developed bureaucracies which had a valuable degree of independence of politicians from the beginning of the nineteenth century, and Britain from the middle of it. Unfortunately, Bismarck began the reversal of this trend (Sheehan 1978, 188) and this culminated when the social classes from which independent-minded civil servants had been drawn were largely destroyed by World War I and the hyper-inflation which followed it (Kingston 1983).

The United States moved towards independence for its civil servants much later, and its 'spoils system' was only gradually rooted out by the Progressive coalition whose agenda was essentially Woodrow Wilson's 1887 article on 'The Study of Administration.' What eventually reversed the trend towards bureaucratic independence there was Roosevelt's New Deal policies, as the quarter-million civil servants hired to carry these through were strongly politicized.

At the limit, lack of civil service independence of politicians can be responsible for actual 'administrative evil' (cf. Adams and Balfour 1998; Moreno-Riaño

2001). How, for example, did the Prussian imperial bureaucracy, built on the ethical foundations of Huguenot immigrants and described by Schumpeter as 'supremely efficient, quite above temptation, entirely independent of politics' (1939, 346) turn into the totally subservient and evil civil service of the Nazi regime? What does the report of the Challenger spacecraft disaster tell about how contemporary civil servants behave when a conflict between duty and career arises? Or the many recent European studies of bureaucratic failures, such as the Matrix-Churchill and 'mad cow' cases in Britain, deaths from contaminated blood transfusions in France as well as Ireland, and the corrupt behaviour which led to the enforced resignation of an entire European Commission?

The reform of modern bureaucracies so that they can play their important role in articulating the public good, independently of wealth and politics, must therefore include strengthened rights for civil servants, like the protection for whistleblowers suggested in the earlier *Studies* and *Political Quarterly* articles. Alternative kinds of reform, which try to make public administration mimic private sector efficiency on the basis of 'technical rationality,' are quite secondary in importance to this. And the start of the process of reform must be to focus attention on getting the laws right as a direct replacement of policies of intervention.

References

Adams, Guy B. and Danny L. Balfour (1998): *Unmasking Administrative Evil*. Thousand Oaks, CA. Sage Publications.

Butler, H. N. (1986): 'General Incorporation in Nineteenth Century England: Interaction of Common Law and Legislative Practices.' *International Review of Law and Economics* 6, 169-187.

French, E. A. (1990) 'The Origin of General Liability in the United Kingdom,' *Accounting and Business Research* 21, pp. 15-34.

Gawthrop, Louis C. (1998): *Public Service and Democracy*. New York. Chatham House Publishers.

Glackin, J. A. (1991): Chestvale Properties and Hoddle Investments Ltd. Interim Report to the Minister for Industry and Commerce. Dublin, the Stationery Office.

Glackin, J. A. (1993): Chestvale Properties and Hoddle Investments Ltd. Final Report to the Minister for Industry and Commerce. Dublin, the Stationery Office.

Kingston, W. (1983): 'Ideas, Civil Servants and Keynes.' *Economic Affairs*, January

- (2001): 'What Can We Do About the Civil Service?' *Studies*, Winter.

- (2002): 'A Running Repair for the Civil Service.' *Political Quarterly*, March.

Mill, John Stuart ([1862] 1994): *Principles of Political Economy*. Book II, Ch. I. London, Longman.

Moreno-Riaño, Gerson (2001): 'The Etiology of Administrative Evil: Eric Voegelin and the Unconsciousness of Modernity.' *American Review of Public Administration* 31: 296-312.

Newman, Bruce L. (1999): *The Mass Marketing of Politics*. Thousand Oaks, CA. Sage Publications.

Nowotny E. (2004) 'Evolution of Structures of European Economic Policy' *J. Evol. Econ.* 14, 211-214

Olson, Mancur (1965): *The Logic of Collective Action: Public Goods and the Theory of Groups*. New York. Schocken Books.

Schumpeter J.A. ([1918] (1991): *The Crisis of the Tax State*. English translation in Swedberg R (ed) *The Economics and Sociology of Capitalism*. Princeton University Press.

- (1939) *Business Cycles*. London, McGraw-Hill.

- ([1943] 1958) *Capitalism, Socialism and Democracy*. London, Allen and Unwin.

Sheehan, James J. (1978): *German Liberalism in the Nineteenth Century*. University of Chicago Press.

Chapter IX
A Patent System To Suit Ireland?
(First published 1987)

Introduction

In recent years there have been increasing misgivings about the way the international patent system has developed. The system is intended to protect innovation, but it has evolved so that it now protects this only indirectly. Patents now protect inventions and in many industrial sectors the linkage between inventions and innovations is weak. The system is also biased against smaller countries such as Ireland and works in favour of the larger countries which are home to most of the leading technological industries. The solution would appear to be to protect innovations *directly*. Proposals for doing this have been discussed in an EEC report, *Direct Protection of Innovation*, and its more important findings are discussed in this article.

Evolution of Patents

The EEC study has special relevance to industrial development in smaller countries. Its origins lie in dissatisfaction about the way in which the international Patent system performs. In a study for the U.S. Senate, the economist Fritz Machlup reported, not very helpfully, that if no patent system existed, it would be a mistake to establish one, but since we do have it we may as well keep it going. A British investigation by Taylor and Silberston concluded that the interest of the United Kingdom in preserving the existing international patent system was no more than 'modest but perceptible'. An official 1976 Canadian Report concluded that ' ... the country should give serious consideration to the possibility of abandoning the continued maintenance of a patent system in any form'. For Australia, according to a 1982 analysis, 'there is little room for doubt that the benefit-cost ratio of the patent system is negative, or at the very best, in balance.' The reason for this is that only a small fraction of the potential of the principle of patenting (the grant of a monopoly in exchange for socially desirable action) has so far been exploited. This in turn is because patents have developed in ways which protects innovation only indirectly.

An invention is a new idea. An innovation is a new idea turned into concrete reality. Originally, patents protected innovations, but they evolved so that they now protect inventions - even though their express objective is still to facilitate innovation. Since innovations are now only protected indirectly, everything depends upon the strength of the link, and the closeness of the correspondence, between them and their associated inventions. In chemicals, for example, the link is strong and correspondence is close; consequently, direct protection of invention, which is indirect protection of innovation, is effective for such products. For mechanical and electrical products, the link between invention and innovation is weak, and there is only a poor correspondence between what customers actually hand over money for and any invention associated with it. The result is that the protection which innovation receives indirectly, through patent protection only for inventions, can often be worthless.

To illustrate, the chemical composition of every tablet of Valium ever sold, must correspond precisely to the original invention as expressed in the formula in Hoffmann-Laroche's patent. There is only a single way of innovating the "teaching" of this patent, and consequently protecting the "teaching" also protects the commercial result. A contrary example is E.M.I.'s brain-scanner - "the most important advance in diagnostic technology since X-rays." In this case, patents could not prevent five other firms from offering copies within three years, and from driving E.M.I. out of the business altogether within a further four. The protection obtained by the hardware through patent protection of the related "teaching" was ineffective because indirect.

The obvious answer is to protect innovations directly and in recent years there have been two comprehensive proposals for doing this. It is these, and their evaluation by a team of international experts, that make up the E.E.C. study under discussion here. Considering that both proposals were developed quite independently, the amount of common ground between them is quite remarkable. In what follows, their residual technical differences will be ignored and their common basic thrust will be designated as "DPI" (Direct Protection of Innovation).

Ireland and the International Patent System

The Irish Free State passed its first Patents Act in 1927, but this was wholly shaped by an earlier decision taken in 1925 to join the International Convention for the Protection of Industrial Property, generally known as the Paris Convention. Membership of this allows a country to have any type of patent system it wishes, as long as it treats the citizens of any other member country in the same way in respect of patent law as its own nationals. However, speaking to the 1927 Bill, this country's first Minister of Industry and Commerce enunciated a principle which has since been followed assiduously, that "the better way is to legislate all that the Convention seeks to achieve". The result has been a totally uncritical following of the features of the international patent system. These inevitably reflect the interests of the most advanced countries, including the protection of inventions rather than innovations.

Imbalance of Advantages

The original signatories of the Paris Convention in 1883 had broadly similar levels of technology, and the Convention carries an implication that there will be some kind of rough balance for a member between the economic value of the monopolies it grants to foreigners and the value of the patents its own nationals will be entitled to obtain abroad. Empirical research, however, has shown conclusively that in Ireland's case, this balance has been almost totally negative, and that substance has been exchanged for shadow. In 1971 Henry Murdoch demonstrated that whereas many patents which had been obtained in Ireland since the first Patents Act by foreign firms were extremely valuable, Irish inventions patented abroad under the Convention earned little or nothing. In fact, as far as the United States - Ireland balance was concerned, the figure in Murdoch's study for the earnings of the Irish patents in the U.S. was actually zero. Murdoch's work has recently been updated by O'Riordan, who found no significant change in recent years. Work which is using a more sophisticated technique than was available to either of these researchers in now in progress to examine the U.S. - Ireland balance even more closely, but this has so far done nothing to call their conclusions into question in the slightest way.

It could nevertheless be argued that a patent system which is recognisably the same as that available to firms in the more advanced countries is part of the modern infrastructure which is a necessary condition for attracting foreign investment. To throw light on this, Collins studied the patenting performance of all firms with Irish manufacturing subsidiaries over several years. His findings show that, except possibly in the case of chemicals (including pharmaceuticals) the existence of patents has made no difference whatever to decisions whether or not to invest in Ireland. Even in the pharmaceutical case, a much more important factor has been tax freedom on patent royalties (including royalties on foreign patents) since 1973.

The proposals for DPI are intended to supplement, and not to replace, the existing patent system. Consequently, although direct protection is ultimately intended to apply to all types of innovation and not just to technology, it would begin with mechanical and electrical innovations, because it is in respect of these that the classical system works least well. The more important features of DPI and the ways in which it differs from the patent system, are as described below.

Criterion of Novelty

For DPI as proposed, the qualification for protection is simply "non-availability in the ordinary course of trade within the E.E.C." That is, if a product with a particular feature cannot be bought through whatever are the normal channels for that type of product, the investment associated with production to fill that gap will be rewarded by a temporary monopoly of sales of products with the new feature. This will occur even if such a product was already on the market elsewhere, e.g. in the United States, or if the novel aspect had been described in technical literature, or even if someone had made a prototype without proceeding to commercial production within the E.E.C. For DPI, the reward is for *doing* the new thing, not for *teaching* it.

This is in sharp contrast to the classical patent system, which only rewards teaching. Moreover, its criterion of novelty is whether or not the teaching is new in the whole world. An Irish patent, for example, would not be granted if its "teaching" could be shown to exist already in the form of an obscure technical paper, filed in a Japanese public library, never translated into English, and never even heard of in Ireland. Even worse, however, is to come. To be valid, the "teaching" of a classical patent must in addition "not be obvious to one skilled in the relevant Art", meaning that a "mosaic" of several earlier documents can equally deprive the "teaching" of protection.

By adopting these criteria, classical patents have come to cater only for the firms that are at the very leading edge of world technology, since only these will have economically relevant "teachings" that are not anticipated by earlier publication in the scientific literature. Such firms just do not exist in any number in smaller countries. Similarly, the incremental innovations that make money are those that evolve organically out of existing technology and in turn point to the next small adaptive change. As such, they will be "obvious to one skilled in the Art" and consequently unpatentable. The many small improvements in products which are responsible for Japanese market dominance do indeed reflect Japanese capability. But they are also made possible by the vacuum left in the West through this abdication of protection for incremental innovation by the classical patent system.

By using strictly commercial criteria for novelty instead of abstractions, therefore, DPI offers the possibility of protection to firms of the type generally to be found in smaller countries, which may not be world leaders in their fields, but which nevertheless have a capacity for innovation, especially of the incremental type. It also provides Western countries with a means of meeting competition from the Shinto-Confucian world.

Irrevocable Grant

The ostensible object of the patent grant of monopoly is to reduce the uncertainty which surrounds any decision to invest in innovation. Here, the classical patent has the great disadvantage that it can be effectively extinguished by the later discovery of information whose existence at the time of grant had been unknown to any of the parties concerned. Who would invest in speculative drilling for oil if his concession could be revoked as a result of new seismic information becoming available about its geological structure? Yet this is what is effectively being asked of an investor in a classical patent.

DPI, on the other hand, offers one opportunity before grant to competitors and the public at large to contradict an applicant's claim that his subject-matter is "not available in the ordinary course of trade". Once made, however, a grant is irrevocable (unless it has been obtained through fraud) and as such must be a far better basis for investment than any classical patent.

Use of Arbitration

Because a patentee has to protect his grant himself through the legal system, a patent is effectively no more than a licence to litigate, and the value of such a licence depends upon the size of its owner's purse. A small firm's valid patent may be infringed with impunity, simply because it cannot afford to pursue a wealthy opponent through the Courts; a large firm may get valuable protection from a patent that is actually invalid, simply because no one dares to take the risk of challenging it. One assumption on which DPI is based is that the state should take a hand in policing the monopolies it grants. This is not only to ensure justice to poor grantees as well as rich, but because infringement of a grant which has been made for a public purpose, is also an attack upon the state's own social policy; there is an element of lése-majesté about it.

If cash is stolen from a business, the police are there to find the thief and have him punished; if the money is taken by a trick, the Fraud Squad intervenes; if an arsonist burns down the firm's factory and is caught, he may be sent to prison; in a case of piracy of an offshore oil rig, presumably the Navy would act; where industry is protected by tariff barriers, every customs officer has a property-protection function; pirate broadcasters who divert advertising revenue from those who have official radio or TV franchises can be taken to court by the state under the Wireless Telegraphy Acts; the Copyright Acts also provide for initiative by the authorities in case of apparent breach. Why, then, should it only be that part of a firm's property which relates to its efforts at innovation that is denied proper protection by the state?

DPI would change this situation by making arbitration of disputes compulsory and selecting arbitrators *ad hoc* from the business, scientific and academic communities for their knowledge of the state of the relevant art. There could be appeal to the Courts from arbitration, but legal aid would then be available to the party who accepted the arbitrator's decision. No small firm would appeal, because it would not have the resources to do so. Large firms would be extremely reluctant to appeal, as a result of the combination of losing an expert arbitration and having to face an opponent who will now have equal resources for litigation. It is believed that as a result, legal aid would be called for very rarely.

Value to Smaller Firms and Countries

These provisions of DPI provide, for the first time, a secure foundation for investment in innovation by small and medium-sized firms. To the extent that such firms are also characteristic of smaller countries, the latter could anticipate major increases in such investments as a result of introducing DPI.

Although too much is being expected of the smaller firms sector at present, especially in terms of employment, it remains true that there are certain kinds of innovation to which such firms are particularly well suited. One of these is incremental innovation, which, as mentioned earlier, is poorly protected by the classical patent system, but very well protected by DPI. Empirical research in Britain (Storey, 1987) has shown that no less than half of all employment growth from small firms comes from only 4% of them. This suggests that policies in support of the generality of small businesses are futile. Instead, efforts should be directed towards removing obstacles to the growth of the very small group of really dynamic firms. DPI would do this automatically, effectively and at virtually no cost to public finances.

A patent monopoly is now granted almost everywhere for 20 years from application in most E.E.C. countries. This looks like a long period for which to shut out competitors from a market, but nobody minds because the protection given is in fact so poor. Competitors are not really shut out. U.S. research (Levin et al., 1984) indicates that effective duplication of a patented product is possible in less than three years, and will also probably cost less than its innovation did.

The monopoly grants of DPI, however, would be a different matter, partly because of incontestability, partly because of the arbitration provisions and partly because of the use of a "whole information contents" approach in deciding questions of infringement. The DPI grant attaches to all new information contained in the product, even that information which can only be identified with the advantage of hindsight. This stress on hindsight reflects the impossibility (which the classical patent system fails to recognise) of understanding the significance of anything new as long as it is new. Whittle thought that the only use of his jet engine invention for civilian purposes would be in mail-carrying aeroplanes, and even as late as the 1940's, Boeing. Douglas and Lockheed refused to entertain the idea that the general public would ever take to travel by jet aircraft! The marketing aspects of any new idea are particularly hard to foresee. As to the feasibility of this approach, it is noteworthy that those who copy seem to be able to pick out, with lightning speed, anything new in a product to which there is even a whiff of a favourable response from the market. For DPI, therefore, infringement is defined as "causing or attempting to cause, loss of revenue to the protected product, other than by innovation which uses none of the new information that is contained in the protected product."

It is believed that the strength of the resulting monopolies will be acceptable to public opinion, because they will be associated with generally shorter terms than those of classical patents. One possibility is to have three monopoly terms, the longest for radical innovations, the shortest for incremental innovations, and an intermediate term. These represent an effort which has never been made in the classical patent system to match the period during which rewards can be reaped from an investment to the risk originally associated with it.

Irish copying of the features of the international system has included its provision that the monopoly grant carries with it no obligation to manufacture locally. After an initial three year period, if a patent is not being "worked". a compulsory licence may be obtained by a third party. However, the requirement of "working" can be satisfied by importation of a token quantity of goods, and research in a number of countries has shown that the compulsory licence aspect of the patent system is very rarely used.

The difference between this and DPI could not be more marked. Since DPI is concerned with innovation, not invention, its concern is to offer protection to investment to produce new products or products with new features. From a smaller country's point of view. this carries highly attractive implications. The monopoly that is granted relates explicitly to investment, its length is tailored to the risk of that investment, and because the investment relates to innovation it has a good chance of resulting in industries with the power of future growth. Note also that this is perfectly compatible with membership of the Paris Convention, whose 'national treatment' provision requires that a DPI grant, like a patent or trademark, would be equally available to foreigner and native. However, whereas a Japanese firm, for example, can obtain an Irish patent and enjoy its monopoly here by means of imports from Japan, it could only get a DPI monopoly by actual investment to produce in Ireland. This involves no discrimination against the Japanese firm, since DPI imposes an identical obligation on Irish applicants. Its possible beneficial implications for inward foreign investment - as indeed for all investment - will be obvious.

Reciprocal Arrangements

In a second stage, it would be possible for two countries which had introduced DPI to agree that they would endorse each other's monopoly grants. This would correspond to a perceptible tendency in new intellectual property legislation internationally to side-step the provisions of the relevant international Conventions. This is undoubtedly the result of a growing sense of the imbalances resulting from the "national treatment" element of these Conventions, specifically referred to earlier in relation to Ireland and patents. 1984 U.S. legislation extending copyright to semi-conductor chips was expressly drafted outside the main U.S. Copyright Act (with the Japanese in mind) to allow insertion of a provision that protection would only be granted to foreign nationals if their countries gave similar protection to U.S. firms. The unregistered design right which is impending in Britain will also not be available automatically to citizens of Paris Convention member countries, as is the case with protection under the current Registered Designs Act.

As between Ireland and Britain, for example, such reciprocity would mean access on a monopoly basis to a much larger market for a small number of Irish innovating firms, in exchange for giving a small addition to their home market to a larger number of British innovators. Since the size of the market is a major determinant of the viability of innovation, there would appear to be a reasonable balance of advantage under such an arrangement, even as between a small and a large country.

An EEC-wide System

The third stage would be introduction of DPI by the E.E.C. as a whole. In spite of the establishment of the European Patent Office at Munich, the actual monopoly grants of classical patents remain the prerogative of national governments. This compromise could hardly operate in the case of DPI, since the essence of a Community system would appear to be a grant of a Community-wide monopoly, and this in turn seems to demand a unitary examining and granting authority.

Such centralization may appear to hand the advantage over once again to the larger countries, but the actual proposals to the E.E.C. include an important countervailing measure. This is that DPI should only be available in respect of investments in those parts of the Community that currently qualify for regional aid. (The monopoly grants, of course, would be Community-wide in their effect). It is claimed that DPI is in fact a vastly better way of assisting the poorer regions than current Regional Aid schemes. These have been proved to give wretched value for what are now very large amounts of money, whereas DPI would be virtually costless.

The thinking behind this proposed measure is based upon empirical research which shows a strong tendency for innovations to be produced close to the location of their anterior R&D. (Oakey 1979). This is an important reason why economic growth in the E.E.C. tends to concentrate in the "golden triangle" from Milan to Rotterdam. If DPI were only available outside this area, however, it would provide a strong incentive for firms to disperse the initial production of new products or of components for products with new features. Subsequent organic growth of industry in the regions as a result of such dispersion could make a substantial contribution both to regional employment and to the Community's expressed aim of reducing disparities in wealth between its member countries.

Why Wait for the EEC?

Ireland, of course, would then qualify for DPI investment as it now does for regional aid. It should be pointed out, however, that the country does not have to wait for a Community-wide scheme to obtain the benefits of DPI. By far the most important of these is that it is a virtually costless alternative to the interventionist industrial policies whose failure is at long last beginning to be publicly admitted. It is perfectly open to Ireland to establish its own DPI arrangements, and until these were copied in other countries it would have a unique advantage in respect of economic innovation. The proposals in this EEC-sponsored enquiry therefore offer this country a remarkable opportunity at a time when a radical new departure in economic policy is so evidently required.

REFERENCES

Canadian Dept. of Consumer Affairs. Working Paper on Patent Law Revision. 1972.
Collins, Patrick: Unpublished T.C.D. dissertation (M.B.A.) 1983.
Kingston, William (ed.) *Direct Protection of Innovation*, Kluwer Academic Publishers for the Commission of the European Communities, Dordrecht and Boston, 1987.
Irish Senate Debates. Vol 9. cols. 548. 568 (P. McGilligan).

Machlup, Fritz: Study No. 15 for U.S. Senate Judiciary Committee. 1958.

Levin, Klevorick, Nelson & Winter: *Yale University Working Paper on Appropriability.* 1984.

Mandeville, Lamberton & Bishop: Report to the (Australian) Industrial Property Advisory Committee. 1982.

Murdoch, H.J.P.: *Invention and the Irish Patent System.* T.C.D. Administrative Research Bureau, 1971.

Oakey, R. P. et al.. *The Spatial Distribution of British Industrial Innovations.* University of Newcastle upon Tyne, 1979.

O'Riordan, Jonathan: Unpublished T.C.D. student project. 1986.

Storey. David: *Are Small Firms the Answer to Unemployment?* Employment Institute. London, 1987.

Taylor, C.T.: 'Do We Still Need a Patent System?' *Journal of the Chartered Institute of Patent Agents.* 1972-3. p.306.

Chapter X
The Financing of New Businesses
(First published 1989)

If there is to be a private sector at all, it should be a healthy one, and no private sector can be healthy without the constant establishment of businesses that are really new, and not just affiliates of old ones. Familiarity has perhaps blunted our awareness of how right Schumpeter was in the famous passage in which he stresses the necessity of 'the perennial gale of creative destruction'. It is not the day-to-day competition that counts, he points out,

> but the competition from the new commodity, the new technology, the new source of supply, the new type of organization ... which strikes not at the margins of the profits and the outputs of the existing firms, but at their foundations and at their very lives. This kind of competition is as much more effective than the other as a bombardment is in comparison with forcing a door, and so much more important that it becomes a matter of comparative indifference whether competition in the ordinary sense functions more or less promptly; the powerful lever that in the long run expands output and brings down prices is in any case made of other stuff[1].

A cause of stagnation

'Expands output and brings down prices ...' Experience of static output and inflation forces us to look seriously at the possibility that a major cause is precisely the absence of the Schumpeterian 'lever'.

It is altogether naive to think that his second and more important type of competition can be brought to bear without the constant formation of new firms. Established businesses have little to fear from one another - from 'competition in the ordinary sense' as Schumpeter put it. Apart from the inherent tendency amongst businessmen to conspire against the public which Adam Smith recorded, every Marketing course to-day at least indirectly teaches the advantages of 'implicit collusion'. The only effective deterrent against putting up prices, and keeping them up, is the fear of being undercut by a new firm, hungry for business. Managements are only spurred into activity to bring out new products by the fear that if they do not do it, some other firm will. Both deterrent and stimulus are absent unless there is a constant flow of new firms which are founded by new men upon new ideas. But it is precisely this for which it is virtually impossible to obtain

---

[1] Schumpeter, J. A., *Capitalism, Socialism and Democracy* (1942) p.84.

finance any longer. Stagnation, therefore, must be due in significant measure to the reduction of the Schumpeterian gale to a zephyr, or even in some areas of industry, to a flat calm.

Investment in innovation

This lack of finance for genuinely new businesses corresponds to the replacement of investors who are spending their own money, by investment managers who are dealing with that of other people.

The first result of this historical change is a drastic reduction in the number of decision points for investment in new businesses. Because such an investment involves uncertainty, every decision involves an emotional element, and this emotional element can only result in a positive decision (i.e. to make an investment) if there is a sufficiently large number of potential decision-makers. Only then can the emotional factors work for a decision instead of against one. Unless there is empathy between entrepreneur and investor, there will be no investment. Consequently, any individual investor is only capable of investing in a very limited range of projects - those that strike his particular *imagination*. If investment is to be possible across a broad range of projects, therefore, the range of investment 'perceptiveness' must be increased correspondingly. This can only be done by multiplying the number of people who can actually make investment decisions. Reducing the number of decision points, as has been done, must correspondingly reduce the number of decisions to invest in a new business.

Secondly, the more emphasis there is on rationality in decision making - as the 'institutional' element grows - the less this can result in positive decisions under uncertainty, such as decisions to invest in new businesses.

Thirdly, as financial organisations become more bureaucratic, those who succeed in them do so by a learning process that is quite different from that of the characteristic innovator. As more investment decisions fall to be made by people who 'have never done it', the possibility of intuitive backing of the right innovations is lessened. With growing awareness of this the organization then tends increasingly to distance itself from the sort of decision that it senses it cannot make well. This leads to avoidance of projects which involve new businesses.

Fourthly, backing for individuals has virtually disappeared. Yet the empirical evidence is now overwhelming that wherever there is successful innovation, there is always an identifiable individual without whom it would not have happened; even where there is a strong 'team' element, the individual 'leadership' element is even stronger. For every successful firm there is an identifiable founder.

'Third party cover'

All of these factors can be seen at work in the way financial Institutions shape up to the financing of new businesses to-day.

This activity shares the characteristic of all innovation that in any single instance, failure is more likely than success, although success, when it comes, is likely to be big. By definition, a hired investment manager will not share proportionately in the few large successes which balance the many failures; whereas he must always fear the effect on his career of association with the failures. Consequently, whereas the dominant question for someone investing his own money is 'how much will this make if it succeeds?', for a hired investment manager what matters is 'how well am I personally 'covered' if it fails?' 'Cover' replaces 'profit' as the criterion for investment. Inevitably, this changes the investment pattern so that failures that can be attributed to individuals are fewer. It so happens that all the means of bringing about this change militate against financing the establishment of new businesses. They include:

i. Setting a minimum level for investment that makes every decision a Committee one. (Most new businesses in fact need relatively small amounts of money, well within the limit of individual 'signatures' in many Banks.)

ii. Setting a minimum level of profit on the part of a business before it will be considered for equity investment (£50,000 a year pre-tax appears to be the generally accepted level amongst Merchant Banks).

iii. Refusal to back individuals. (Every genuinely new business, even when it starts with a team, will have a single moving spirit).

iv. 'Third party cover', obtained by shunting commercial and technical responsibility on to a firm with assets and a reputation. (Obviously, insistence as a condition of financing that an established firm be involved in a joint venture, means that whatever comes out of the decision cannot be a genuinely new and competitive business).

'The loneliness of the hired investment manager'

It is easy to illustrate all these tendencies even from the institutions which have been set up specifically to fill the vacuum left by the decline of the individual investor.

It cannot be stressed too strongly that the fact that this is possible does not reflect in the slightest way upon the ability or integrity of the executives of these organisations. But nothing can change the reality that they are not spending their own money, and the way in which they dispose of the money entrusted to them, must reflect their career situations. Anything else would be quite irrational on their part. One such institution has met the problem of investing money at high risk by adopting as formal policy, 'backing firms, not individuals'. From its point of view, this at least means that it can escape the worst hazards of start-up financing. The annual reports of a second institution record a constantly growing proportion of joint ventures with established industry in its total activity. In fact, its typical 'favourable' response to an applicant is 'if you succeed in interesting a substantial Company, then the question of our participation could be considered'. A third, established for the financing of businesses in their early stages, is recorded in published data as completing only 4 investments in 2 years, although it is strongly financed.

Of the various factors involved, it is 'Third Party Cover' which best corresponds to 'the loneliness of the hired investment manager'. 'If "A" couldn't make a success of it, nobody could' or 'we could reasonably have supposed that "Y" would get the export markets', or 'Z' are the technical experts; we're only financial men', are all related to investment decisions which such a manager can take without the danger of damaging his career path within an Institution. But it is also 'Third Party Cover' that has the most damaging economic consequences. It means the replacement of profit as the criterion of investment in innovation, which can only mean that the ideas actually innovated will be the economically second-rate ones. The historic decline in the profitability of industry can only reflect in some manner the resulting misallocation of resources in the face of competition from innovating industries abroad which have kept the profit measure.

Worse still, 'Third Party Cover' means that the decision as to what innovations there will be, is effectively abdicated by the Institutions set up specifically to facilitate innovation, and passed to established firms. Even the best of these will be the worse for not having to withstand the gale of creative destruction, whilst the worst are thus enabled to survive in senility long after their creative spark is extinguished. Nothing concentrates the mind of management more wonderfully than the thought that rejecting a new idea may not be enough to prevent it from coming to life in the hands of another; but if the Institutions will only contribute their support within the context of established firms, then these firms are denied this most valuable stimulus.

Also, if the top management of a firm can be virtually sure that there is no chance of people lower down finding finance to get out and do it themselves if their ideas are not taken up, then it is under correspondingly less pressure to do something about their new ideas. And the time-scale of innovations is such that it is rarely possible to pin the blame for misused chances on anyone. By the time the Boeing Hydrofoil speeds up the Thames, those who denied support to Christopher Hook's vision are in retirement, full of years and honours.

Suggested policies

As far as new businesses are concerned, therefore, current institutional arrangements are quite inadequate substitutes for the system they replace. What can be done to improve them?

In the first place, there is no point in establishing yet another Institution. Since this would also have to be staffed by hired managers, their loneliness in decision-making would be no different from their fellows in the existing Institutions, and they too would soon run for the same kind of cover.

Equally, without assistance and stimulus from the State, there is at present no possibility of obtaining the results required from the privately owned Institutions on their own. For a start, they are disillusioned with investment in any kind of innovation. The 30 Banks and Insurance Companies that originally invested in Technical Development Capital had to share a large loss before it was taken over by ICFC. Worse, European Enterprises Development SA, in which 17 Banks, including the Midland, had shares, and which had most prestigious management and associates, actually failed recently. And the fact that the name of the Bank that originally backed Whittle's jet engine is no longer to be found in the Banker's Almanac is only one of the horror stories about innovation in the City's folklore, almost all of them true.

In the United States, the Small Business Administration is empowered to lend up to 4 times their own capital to firms which invest in or lend to businesses with assets up to $9 million and profits, after tax, up to $400,000 per annum. This, and other provisions of the 1958 Act, have been very effective in second and third-stage financing, but something more is required to deal with the problem of 'start-up' financing.

What is proposed, therefore, is a mixture of state and private financing for new business which would have the effect of:-

i. Reducing the risk in an individual investment decision to the level that makes such a decision possible for a hired manager.

ii. Multiplying the number of decision points.

iii. Outlawing 'Third Party Cover' as a means of avoiding decisions.

All these objectives could be met by a scheme whereby the National Enterprise Board (or Equity Capital for Industry) was empowered to provide a multiple of the venture capital invested in a new enterprise in which a 'participating' Merchant Bank was involved.

To participate in the scheme, such a Bank would have to commit itself to invest a specified but very small proportion of its total lendings over a period, in new businesses as defined. Once holding participant status, however, the Bank would automatically have access to a multiple of its own money, for the same project, to be invested on the same terms. NEB/ECI would not be responsible for any technical or commercial evaluation of a project. All they would have to do is ensure that the Bank in question had made its own equity investment. Funds from outside individual shareholders could count towards the Bank's 'quota' and for 'multiple' matching. A fundamental part of the definition of a 'new business' for the purpose of the scheme would be that it could have no corporate shareholder other than a financial one.

In this scheme, the 'multiple' meets objective (i), by introducing a type of 'gearing' for risk capital in new businesses. The multiple could be varied from time to time, according to perceived need for the establishment of new businesses, alternative outlets for their funds open to the Institutions and other factors. To give the scheme a flying start, a multiple of 10 is suggested. It could always be reduced if it is found in practice to be too generous. Use of the Merchant Banks goes a good distance towards objective (ii) initially. Every 1/10 of 1 % of normal UK lendings of the Accepting Houses which was earmarked for 'participation' would produce £1 million for investment in new businesses from this source. (For comparison, NRDC's annual spending is of the order of £6 million and T.D.C's is 1 million). Whatever about the Clearing Banks, there seems no reason why the Insurance Companies, at least the Life Offices, which are in a position to lend long, should not eventually be recruited to the scheme. They might well set up subsidiaries to take advantage of this new form of investment, in much the same way as all types of Financial Institutions set up Small Business Investment Companies in the U.S. to gain the advantage of registration with the Small Business Administration.

Objective (iii) is met by banning corporate shareholders other than financial. Obviously, there would have to be provisions to prevent established firms obtaining back-door entry to the new firms, whether through nominee shareholders or otherwise.

A very minor legislative change would reinforce the effect of this scheme. This would be to permit tax losses to be applied, irrespective of type of business. At present, an established firm can write most of its current investment in innovation off against its tax liability, whereas if a new firm is the vehicle and the project fails, the losses are worthless for tax relief except to a firm in the same line of business. If this restriction was removed, a wider market in tax loss Companies would develop, with the result that investors could reasonably expect some degree of mitigation of any terminal losses. This would put existing business and new business on a more equal tax footing as vehicles for investing in innovation, and by reducing the risk of a new business somewhat, would lower a barrier to investment correspondingly.

In the long run, the effectiveness of the scheme will of course depend upon a legal - especially tax - regime which does not penalise newly established firms in their early days. Amplification of the above comments can be found, if needed, in the author's Invention and Monopoly[2] and Innovation: the Creative Impulse in Human Progress[3].

---

[2] Woolwich Economic Paper No. 14.

[3] New Edition, 2003. Washington, D.C. L. F. Sugerman Press.

Chapter XI
Nice Rents If You Can Get Them

In updating this collection of ideas, a useful beginning can be made with those in the Chapters on 'Belief in the Superior Wisdom of the State' and 'The Lemmings of Democracy.' These deal with different aspects of the tension between the public good and individual interests which is endemic to democratic societies. The debates around the drafting of the Constitution of the United States, which can be regarded as the Charter of democracy in its modern form, reflect this tension and the problems that arise from it, and can also cast light on the evolution of Irish policies.

The Framers of that Constitution had a vision of a government that would act for the public good, but they feared that it could be captured by 'faction,' or what today would be called 'special interest' or 'vested interest' groups. This is why they were so concerned, as Thomas Jefferson put it, 'that the powers of government ... be so divided and balanced among several bodies of magistracy, as that no one could transcend their legal limits, without being effectively checked and restrained by the others'.[1]

Modern experience in all democracies shows how right the Framers of the Constitution were to be afraid of 'faction.' Their fear was of what Jefferson called 'elective despotism' (that is, voters acting solely in their own interest with no concern for the public good). What they could never have envisaged was the growth of faction in the form of corporate power to influence electors and politicians in the first instance, and through them, legislation which delivers privileges. Business in its corporate form became general only from the mid-nineteenth century, but its influence increased enormously throughout the twentieth, a trend which was noted as long ago as 1962 by Buchanan and Tullock:

> We may observe a notable expansion in the range and extent of collective activity over the last half-century—especially in that category of activity appropriately classified as differential or discriminatory legislation. During the same period we

---

[1] Thomas Jefferson, Note on the State of Virginia ed. Peden, William 1982: Chapel Hill, University of North Carolina Press, 120; quoted in Lazare, Daniel 2001: The Velvet Coup: the Constitution, the Supreme Court and the Decline of American Democracy, London, Verso.

have witnessed also a great increase in investment in organized interest-group efforts designed specifically to secure political advantage.[2]

The record in the United States shows that after about its first century and a half, laws increasingly tended to be shaped by those who could benefit from them. In particular, since Buchanan and Tullock wrote, the coming of television has increased the cost of getting elected by an order of magnitude. This forces politicians to be correspondingly more responsive to those who can finance their campaigns, and makes the Framers' careful checks and balances in the U.S., and copies of them in other countries, ineffective.

A world-wide phenomenon

This is happening everywhere. Chapter 1 cited a Vice-President of the European Investment Bank who wrote when he was reviewing his ten-year period of office recently, that 'Policy in Brussels thus has evolved from a European-encompassing institutions approach to a U.S.-Style "special interest" approach...'[3]

Such a shift is perhaps the most virulent of what Robert Skidelsky (see Chapter 1) called 'the pathologies which deform, and at the limit destroy...political economies.' Or, as the great Austrian economist and sociologist, Joseph Schumpeter, put it, 'It is part of the State's nature that it opposes individual egoism as a representative of a common purpose. Only then is it a separate, distinguishable social entity.'[4] When interests have made the State largely indistinguishable from themselves, government justifies Marx's taunt that it is 'nothing more than the Committee of the bourgeoisie.' Worse, interests that have captured the State are themselves unable to sustain it in time of trouble. Gibbon wrote of the oligarchs who dominated the later Roman empire that they would not fight to save it from the barbarians, because they did not believe that they deserved their wealth. Closer to ourselves, John Maynard Keynes observed of the aftermath of World War I that

> We are thus faced in Europe with the spectacle of an extraordinary weakness on the part of the great capitalist class, which has emerged from the industrial triumphs of the nineteenth century, and seemed a very few years ago our all-powerful master. The terror and personal timidity of the individuals of this class is now so great, their confidence in their place in society and in their necessity to the social organ-

---

[2] Buchanan, James M. and Gordon Tullock, 1962: *The Calculus of Consent*, Ann Arbor, University of Michigan Press, 269.

[3] Nowotny, E.: 'Evolution of structures of European economic policy', Journal of Evolutionary Economics, 14, 2004, 211–4.

[4] Schumpeter, Joseph A. 1918: 'The Crisis of the Tax State'. English translation in Swedberg, R. (ed.) 1991: *The Economics and Sociology of Capitalism*. New York, Harper and Row, 110.

ism so diminished, that they are the easy victims of intimidation... Perhaps it is historically true that no order of society ever perishes save by its own hand.[5]

Irish vulnerability to 'faction'

In the Irish case, as discussed in Chapter II, the electoral system makes politicians exceptionally vulnerable to interests, and the revelations of the McCracken, Moriarty and Flood/Mahon tribunals have put this beyond argument. It might be suggested that in the property-rights/numbers balance, the more wealth gains control over politicians, the more the extra power which proportional representation gives to numbers is needed. This would indeed be the case, if the two elements in the balance were genuinely separated from each other. In fact, the way in which those with wealth obtain their influence over political parties is through funding their campaigns, that is, to help them persuade 'numbers' against those 'numbers' own interests. If strict limits on payments to parties could be laid down and enforced, proportional representation might indeed assist in counterbalancing interests, whereas without such limits it leaves people even more vulnerable to interests than other voting arrangements do. As things stand, rent-seeking rules in Ireland: clientelism and unproductive public sector growth are two sides of the same coin.[6]

It was pointed out in Chapter II that in the property/numbers balance, it is only independent property that counts. Of course, this means only property that is owned by those who live and work in a country. The large amount of property in Ireland that belongs to multinational corporations only constrains governments to the extent that they are encouraged to avoid policies which will cause these footloose entities to leave the country, with consequent unemployment. Nor does the wealth of Irish tax exiles, much of which in any event has originated in successful rent-seeking as part of 'faction,' count in the equation. Another element that is unique in the Irish democratic balance, and which can be expected to grow in importance, is the ability of one political party to obtain substantial funding outside the country, which must force other parties into a race to the bottom on the 'numbers' side.

One important change since 'The Lemmings of Democracy' was published is the influence of the EU, which is now the source of at least two-thirds of Irish legislation, and which mitigates the harm of the proportional representation system. A country which could put on its official website the names of the corpo-

---

[5] Keynes, J. M. 1920: *The Economic Consequences of the Peace*. London, Macmillan, 222.

[6] See Piattoni, Simona, ed., 2001: *Clientelism, Interests and Democratic Representation*. Cambridge, University Press.

rate sponsors of its 6-months Presidency of the European Commission, shows how blind those who run it are to the essential distinction between business and politics. Without the EU constraint, for example, there would surely have been capitulation to local interests in respect of salmon drift netting, with the inevitable result of total destruction of the resource. Nevertheless, the EU's influence has been anything but benign in other ways. Its own common fisheries policy is a disaster, and its funding has greatly increased the opportunities for rent-seeking, as discussed in earlier Chapters.

Countervailing factors

Since 'faction' is so strong in Ireland, are there any 'bodies of magistracy' available to 'check and restrain' it? Or to help the State 'oppose individual egoism as a representative of a common purpose'? In theory, a permanent civil service ought to be a powerful counterbalance to the influence of interests and the venality of politicians, and indeed this has actually been the reality in some countries in the past. International organizations use how independent of politics its civil service is, as an indicator of the quality of a country's governance.[7]

In Ireland, corruption began later in national than in local government, and the conditions in the Treaty for manning a permanent civil service must be given much of the credit for this. These conditions did not apply to Corporations and County Councils, however, where one of the first consequences of Independence was dismissal of all the senior officials who were in post under the 1908 Act. The Local Appointments Commission then had to be established as early as 1924 because of the level of bribery associated with the appointments these bodies were making. This corruption grew to the extent that it eventually became necessary to take many powers away from the local authorities and have them exercised instead by City and County Managers. Even after that, the way in which the notorious 'Section 140' motions and other devices have been used to defeat proper planning, teach sad lessons about the meaning of 'faction.'

Unfortunately, at the national level, at the same time as interests have been consolidating their grip on politicians, the evolution of the Irish civil service has been in the direction of making it more compliant with the wishes of its political masters, even when these wishes are opposed to the public good and can be clearly seen to be so. This service was never shaped by the religious ethic of the Prussian one, which was staffed at the top by Huguenot exiles from France. Nor were its members prepared for serving in it by anything like the French Grandes

---

[7] See for example: www.worldbank.org/wbi/governance/govdata.

Ecoles or the public school system in Britain. It was a clone of the British system, set down in a significantly different culture.

Civil service governance

That culture was not long in bringing about change in the system, as is illustrated in the career of Joseph Brennan, the earliest Secretary of the Department of Finance. He was an Irish member of the British service who was one of those sent to Dublin before World War I to prepare the Castle for the coming into effect of the Home Rule Act. The system that formed him had emerged out of the Trevelyan-Northcote reforms of 1852. These established a threefold division: Administrators, Executives and Technical people. Administrators were University-educated, and were recruited through a special examination; Executives were school-leavers, and technical people were those who had particular necessary qualifications. The members of the two latter groups were never expected to rise to the top posts, so the Administrative class was in effect the officer corps of the civil service.

It was natural for Brennan to try to shape the Irish civil service so that only those who had entered at the administrative level would be eligible to be promoted to the higher posts. However, he encountered strong opposition from those who had entered as executives and was eventually defeated.[8] There are some indications that more of those who get promoted to the top ranks in the Irish civil service, other than in Foreign Affairs, have tended to enter at the lower educational level. However small a difference this elimination of a formal officer corps has made, it is one that inevitably works towards making the civil service more pliable in the hands of Ministers.

Brennan himself was anything but pliable in respect of the behaviour of his own Minister, whose 'solo runs' traduced everything he had been trained to understand about the proper relationship between politicians and the civil service. Consequently, he resigned, eventually being compensated under a provision of the 1920 Government of Ireland Act which covered civil servants 'whose position might be rendered intolerable.'[9]

A politicised bureaucracy

Many civil servants admit the increased politicisation of Irish bureaucracy in recent years, but put the blame on the introduction of Ministerial special advisors. It is of course understandable that permanent officials should be unhappy at the

---

[8] Fanning, Ronan 1978: *The Irish Department of Finance 1922-1958*, Dublin, Institute of Public Administration, 542

[9] O'Broin, Leon, 'Joseph Brennan, Civil Servant Extraordinary.' *Studies* (1977) 25-37.

change from the earlier situation when they were the sole source of expert advice on which a politician could call, but it is going too far to lay the decline in independence of the civil service at the door of the new advisory system. Many other factors have been involved, of which three are readily identifiable: Limiting the term of office of departmental heads; changing the system for making top appointments; and the belief that bureaucratic efficiency can be achieved by importing management techniques from the private sector.

Bringing in a limit of seven years for the tenure of office by a Departmental head was probably an aspect of the 'management techniques' belief, in which such an appointee would allegedly be able to perform like a Chief Executive Officer in the business world. But it also corresponds with the self-interest of ambitious civil servants.

It has been altogether pernicious. Formerly, joining the civil service meant a lifetime commitment, with no expectation of appointments after retirement. These conditions equipped those who rose to the top with quite a degree of resistance to manipulation by politicians or bribery through prospects offered by business men. For example, Sir Warren Fisher, who did so much to foster the new Irish State, was Head of the British civil service from 1919 up to the outbreak of war in 1939, and his namesake in the Admiralty, 'Jackie' Fisher, turned down an offer of a salary of no less than £10,000 a year (a prodigious sum at the end of the nineteenth century) from an armaments firm.

The situation in Ireland now is very different, as the post-civil service careers of some recent Secretaries-General indicate. So much so, that the objective of a career in the Service, which used to be said to be 'the security,' has now become 'the jobs after retirement' for the most ambitious. For the top people who must now retire after comparatively few years, this can mean new and lucrative careers starting in their 'fifties. Consequently, none of these can be indifferent during their time in post, to the wishes of Ministers who hold appointments to lucrative quangos in their gift, or to those of powerful business men with whom they come into contact, irrespective of what the public good might require. It would be surprising if they were not compliant, and their example infects their subordinates and destroys what should be a crucial element in defending the polity against its capture by interests.

One of the British enquiries into the origins of the Iraq War showed how the ambition of the Chairman of the Joint Intelligence Committee (JIC) to become the head of the Secret Intelligence Services, could have led to the Prime Minister being told what he wanted to hear, instead of being given the much more nuanced information which the Committee actually had. Lord Butler and his colleagues reported that there was a strong case that the post of Chairman of the JIC should never again be held by anyone other than an official 'who is demonstrably beyond influence, and thus probably in his last post.[10]

The problem in Ireland is that there is now no such thing as a 'last post' in this sense for the top civil servants, because of the combination of retirement at a comparatively young age with opportunities for new careers in the gift of Ministers or business men. Enquiry after enquiry has made it abundantly clear that many senior civil servants have been anything but 'demonstrably beyond influence.'

The civil servant as courtier

It will of course be argued that civil servants should not be restricted in how they earn their livings, any more than other persons. In a free economy, that would be unanswerable, because any jobs offered to retired civil servants would be on a basis of proven skills and abilities. That is not the case in Ireland, which is so committed to intervention in the economy. The more the civil service proves its inability to handle such interventions, the more of them have to be hived off, which provides opportunities for Ministers to appoint trusted ex-civil servants to run them. Correspondingly, an interventionist economy opens up so many possibilities for rent-seeking, that retired senior civil servants are sought by business men, not for their skills, but for their knowledge of how the system works and their relationships with former colleagues and politicians. In influencing both groups, nothing is more valuable than knowing where bodies are buried.

In Chapter VI it was stressed that the task of his or her Department must always take second place to an individual's career path within the bureaucracy. Given future prospects outside the civil service for those on the higher rungs of the promotion ladder, nothing is easier to see that Ministers' wishes, whether spoken or unspoken, will be energetically complied with throughout such a career path.

As part of attempts to 'modernise' the civil service, an arrangement for making top appointments by an external Committee was set up, and it originally recommended only a single name for an appointment. However, in 1997, this was changed to three names. Obviously, this greatly increases Ministerial influence in the selection process, which in turn must make ambitious civil servants correspondingly more compliant with their wishes.

It is not fanciful, indeed, to suggest that Irish higher civil servants have deci-

---

[10] www.butlerreview.org.uk at paragraph 597.

sively moved in the direction of being courtiers in the service of Ministerial mon-archies. The fiction of the Minister as completely responsible for what happens in a 'Corporation sole' makes him a king within his Department. The jobs to which civil servants aspire are the counterparts to the offices and monopolies which place-seekers and functionaries sought from royal favours, in the days before monarchies became Constitutional, with civil services independent of them.

'What a bureaucracy can and cannot do'

It is precisely because of its independence of politics that a civil service, which in its modern form is a creation of the nineteenth century, is different from a Court. To use Jefferson's phrase, it is a new 'body of magistracy.' But in contemporary Ireland, Ministers who are part of a government which is ultimately dependent upon votes cast under proportional representation, will always be anxious to in-tervene in the economy, and to take initiatives which can gain them publicity. To the extent that higher civil servants understand what a bureaucracy is, and what it can and cannot do, they should resist many such initiatives because they are be-yond the capacity of a civil service to do well, and sometimes even to do at all.

If, on the other hand, they have come to think, not as civil servants, but as courtiers, still more if they have also come to believe that the capacity to manage can be attained by learning some techniques, they are more likely to take on the tasks imposed upon them by politicians, instead of resisting them. The wish of higher civil servants to show that they can 'manage' has led many Irish civil ser-vice departments into a quagmire of tasks characterised by a scope and complex-ity that they are incapable of mastering. Attempts to mimic what works in private industry have failed, because they necessarily leave out the crucial element of individual responsibility.

The fantasy that higher civil servants can be managers in the sense of pri-vate enterprise – even the worst large-scale, bureaucratic private enterprise – has caused them to flounder into debacle after debacle. There is simply no compari-son between their employment conditions and those where market forces are de-livering genuine competition. When asked how he chose his generals, Napoleon is said to have replied: 'I leave it to the god of battles.' The same god is in charge of selection in businesses which have to compete to survive. Individual managers carry responsibility for departments or projects over significantly long periods, and the ones who get promotion are those who win the battles which have to be fought. Poor managers are eliminated, because firms which leave them in post go to the wall themselves, and the threat of this is always present to them. To quote Schumpeter yet once more, 'The competition that counts is...the competition which strikes not at the margins of profit and the outputs of the existing firms, but at their very lives.'[11]

Avoiding blame

There is no competition to 'strike at the very life' of a State bureaucracy, so the 'god of battles' does not choose those who get to the top in it. Avoidance of attributable failure is what counts instead, and the main techniques for achieving this are the proliferation of committees and mobility of individuals. These mechanisms ensure that no individual can be blamed for the failure of projects. They are especially useful for avoiding blame when compliance with Ministers' wishes has led a Department to undertake tasks of a kind which simply could not be carried through without individual commitment and leadership over a long period.

There is no shortage of examples of the inability of Departmental heads to resist involving their staff in politically-inspired lost causes, simply because their environment is one which is designed to ensure that no insider loses, but only the public. The enquiry into the Department of Health's disastrous computer system shows the people supposedly in charge constantly moving to different posts, and the personnel of Committees constantly changing, so that individuals can escape blame for the mess which they leave behind, which consequently becomes worse and worse.[12] The readiness of the Department of the Environment, Heritage and Local Government to comply with its Minister's wish to introduce electronic voting in a hurry, when there had been 'no independent end-to-end testing of the full system as it would be operated at elections,' would have been out of the question if individuals had to be ready to accept blame for failure.[13] Any private firm which acted in this way would quickly disappear.[14]

British Petroleum's recent history illustrates this point. Its reputation for high quality of management has been greatly tarnished by the U.S. Government's enquiry into an explosion at one of its refineries at which a number of employees were killed. The cause of this was poor equipment maintenance, which in turn is now blamed on the reduction in the length of time a BP manager stays in one post before moving on to another one. There has also been reduction in length of job tenure in the higher grades of the Irish civil service, probably to a greater extent even than in BP. Since this has been accompanied by a huge widening in the

---

[11] Schumpeter, J. A. (1943): *Capitalism, Socialism and Democracy*. London, Allen and Unwin, 84.

[12] See http://audgen.gov.ie/documents/vfmreports/VFM_51_PPARS_Report.pdf

[13] See http://www.ccv.ie/htm/report/first_report/part4_3.htm

[14] For the slipshod way in which a Government Department puts together and implements what it calls a 'business plan,' see http://www.oireachtas.ie/documents/committees29thdail/pacdocuments/6th_Report_2003.pdf

range and complexity of the tasks these civil servants undertake, it is inevitable that management without responsibility becomes the norm, making failure of the tasks inevitable.

As noted in Chapter I, Government's experience with these failures has led them to turn to public-private partnerships as a way of spending public money less wastefully. However, as also noted in that Chapter, facing entrepreneurs for whom taking responsibility is a way of life with civil servants whose environment requires them to evade responsibility as far as they possibly can, is an unequal contest which can only result in further growth in rent-seeking.

The Cromien and Sullivan Reports

Constantly changing committee membership and mobility of personnel to evade responsibility also explain the quite extraordinary inability of the civil service to learn from its errors. In 1996, for example, the Department of Justice failed to advise a judge of the Special Criminal Court when his tenure had come to an end, with the result that he continued to act, making the resulting decisions of the Court illegal. The Cromien report into how this happened revealed a pathetic level of competence on the part of highly-paid individuals, with letters left unanswered, information not passed on, no-one taking responsibility for anything.[15]

It might have been expected that a Department which had been held up to public ridicule for this kind of incompetence would take special care with its internal communications afterwards. Yet these failed a second time in the Brendan Smith case which brought down a government, after which special arrangements were put in place to ensure it could not happen again. In spite of this, almost unbelievably, the same inability to get even the simplest elements of internal communication right has been confirmed for yet a third time – 'on several occasions' - in the Sullivan report into the case which led to the declaration of unconstitutionality of the statutory rape law.[16]

One of the most egregious examples of the supine nature of senior civil servants in the face of political pressure is the behaviour of the Revenue Commissioners, as this has emerged from the Moriarty Report. Admittedly, this was during what the judge described as 'a dismal period in the interface between politics and business in our recent history,'[17] when many institutions of the State were being corrupted by unprecedented bullying from the political centre. These Commissioners do not have the Constitutional status of the Comptroller and Audi-

---

[15] See Feldman, Estelle, 'Accountability: a Case Study,' *Studies* 1999, 140-153.

[16] Key points of this report are in: http://www.taoiseach.gov.ie/index.asp?docID=2770

[17] Report of the Tribunal of Enquiry into Payments to Politicians and Related Matters Part I, 547.

tor-General (in fact, nobody seems to know exactly where they fit into the civil service system) but they nonetheless rank very close to the top. What possible view of the dignity of his Office, then, could be that of a Chairman of this body who acted on the instigation of a bribed politician to bring about 'nothing short of a complete turn round in the consistent thinking of Revenue'[18] in respect of a massive tax liability? And then, after retirement, to put himself – 'entirely inappropriately'[19] - in the pay of the beneficiary for what he himself accepted was 'a very large fee for the research undertaken'?[20]

An aspect of the Moriarty account of this affair which is particularly worth noting, is the way in which officials lower down in the hierarchy so readily ('assiduously' is the word used by the judge) acquiesced in the procedures whereby this tax liability was reduced by about the equivalent of €30 million, once they sensed their Chairman's altered stance in the matter. Only one of them dissented ('vigorously') from their failure to appeal a decision of the Appeals Commissioners to the Court. With a whistleblowing regime such as suggested in Chapters VI and VII, that individual might have been able to prevent the entire blatant breach of procedures; even more important, the fear that this could happen might have put some backbone into the Chairman at the outset.

The disease of organizational cohesion

Civil servants who took the trouble to respond to Chapters VI and VII when they were originally published were at one in opposing the proposals for whistleblowing. One considered that the problems were too deep-seated to be effectively dealt with in this way.[21] Another argued that there are many good civil servants, loyally doing their jobs as best they can, and that whistleblowing would introduce a factor which could potentially damage their relationships. It is important to distinguish between individual goodness and diseased institutions – think of Keynes's comment before he resigned from the British delegation to the Versailles Peace Treaty: 'I work for a government I despise for ends I think criminal.'[22] Recently, the Home Secretary in Britain described his Department as 'not fit for purpose,' which is a perfect description of what a diseased organization is, yet no doubt there are many good people in that Department, too, 'loyally doing their jobs as

---

[18] ibid. 601

[19] ibid. 394

[20] ibid. 361

[21] Prior, Michael: 'A Response to William Kingston,' *Studies* (2001) 449.

[22] Keynes, J. M. (1917) Letter to Duncan Grant, 15 December. British Museum Add. MSS 57931 fo. 119.

best they can.' Relationships, comradeship, solidarity, *esprit de corps*, collegiality, the cohesion which holds an organization together, can all be beneficial, even essential, but like everything else, they can become corrupted. Every disease has its own pathology, or the way in which it reveals its presence, and the pathology of diseased organizational cohesion is the cover-up. This is why Chapter VI claimed that 'the cover-up is the besetting sin of bureaucracy.'

Some groups, such as armies and police forces, are particularly vulnerable to this type of corruption, because the nature of their work requires that their members need exceptionally strong cohesive bonds. When your life may depend upon your comrades, of course you will be ready to 'circle the wagons' to defend them against outsiders, however much in the wrong they may be. But unless this readiness to cover up wrong-doing by members of the in-group is controlled, it will eventually make the entire group ineffective. Historically, this has been prevented from happening in the groups most prone to this type of corruption by the device of an officer corps which does not fully share the cohesion of the majority of the group, to limit the cover-up of wrongdoing within that majority. In Ireland, the army has used this device, but, regrettably, the police have not, and the results, as we now know from the reports of Justice Morris, have been disastrous for their reputation.

From its beginnings, the Irish army adopted the arrangements which are characteristic of all established States, in which there is a clear distinction between those whose job it is to command and those who have to obey. The Act which established the Army in 1924 clearly set out that it was to comprise 'officers, non-commissioned officers and men;' the Cadet School was established in 1926, and soon after this young officers began to be sent abroad for training. Of course, the distinction between officers and men has always been a fundamental feature of army life, and insubordination is severely punished.

The Morris Reports

Not so with the Garda Siochana. When it was brought into being to replace the Royal Irish Constabulary (RIC) and the Dublin Metropolitan Police, well over 90% of its recruits had been members of the IRA, subject only to irregular discipline. General O'Duffy, its first Commissioner, saw the need for a corps of specially selected and trained officers, and one of his early actions was to get Cabinet approval to revive the old RIC system, by setting up a cadet school for this purpose. However, this was strongly resented by the rank-and-file gardai. The opposition of their Representative Association ensured that there was only a single entry of cadets, in 1925, from which 39 officers graduated. All of these became superintendents, but that was the end of the attempt to introduce a formal officer corps to the Garda.[23] (There is an evident contemporary parallel between what happened in this case, and formal Garda resistance to the new Reserve force).

In contrast to the Army's officers, therefore, who are a distinct group from the men, and are recruited to be so, the Garda's officers all come up through the ranks. Because of the Morris reports, we now know how much they lack the crucial ability to prevent the corruption of comradeship in the force. We will never know who actually killed Richie Barron in Donegal by running him down, but the balance of probabilities points to the culprit being either a garda or someone that a garda wished to protect. No outsider would have had the means, motive and opportunities to initiate and pursue all the actions (and inactions) which led to charges of murder and complicity in murder being laid against innocent people and pressed most vindictively by the police in a massive series of cover-ups. Throughout the country, the revelations have raised the spectre of how much more wrongdoing could have been successfully covered up by gardai over the years, bringing great harm to innocent people. The phrase 'but who'd know? We'd be in charge' reverberates in a terrifying way. It should be remembered that it was only some quite fortuitous elements that brought garda corruption in Donegal to light.

'Indiscipline and insubordination'

But why were the internal Garda enquiries so ineffectual in dealing with the multiple cover-ups? Appalling as the behaviour of the Donegal gardai was, it is the utter failure of their superiors to make any kind of fist of dealing with it, through three internal 'enquiries,' that is of greatest concern. Justice Morris had to report on 'a staggering level of indiscipline and insubordination in the force;' that rank and file gardai had no compunction about showing contempt for their officers, and 'that the culture of indiscipline was not confined to Donegal but also exists elsewhere.'[24] The answer to the question is because those doing the investigating were not part of an officer corps capable of controlling the corruption of cohesion in a body where comradeship is so important. The crucial distinction between those who set the standards and those who have to work according to those standards did not exist.

The Guards who were being investigated by the force's internal enquiries were on first-name terms with their officers and investigators, which is scarcely surprising, given that they had all been through the same training at Temple-

---

[23] McNiffe, Liam 1977: *A History of the Garda Siochana.* Dublin, Wolfhound Press, 67-69.

[24] See http://www.justice.ie/80256E010039C5AF/vWeb/flJUSQ6SREZX-en/$File/Morris5thRpt.pdf

more. When individuals begin on a basis of equality, it is not easy for any of them, when promoted into authority over the others, to impose that authority, and subordinates can readily flout it. The Garda Commissioner has described the difficulty of imposing sanctions on guards who are clearly in the wrong, because every case is forced through the courts and financed by the Garda equivalents of Trades Unions. This could never have been allowed to become normal practice if there had been a specially recruited and trained officer corps, supervised by a Department of Justice which was doing its job. The efforts at reform which are now under way, in the Ombudsman Commission, the O'Keefe proposals and the like, are all very belated attempts to make up for the frustration of the attempt to introduce such a body in 1925.

'Compassion and collegiality'

A valuable insight into how group cohesion can operate against the public good has been provided by an enquiry into the behaviour of three obstetricians by the Medical Council's Fitness to Practice Committee. The whistle had been blown on the surgical behaviour of a colleague of theirs in Drogheda by two brave mid-wives, and he was threatened with suspension by the North-Eastern Health Board. The Secretary of the Hospital Consultants' Union, Mr. Fitzpatrick, 'pressured' the three to interview this doctor, to study a number of his cases, and to provide him (Fitzpatrick) with a Report which could help to prevent this suspension. Although they admitted that they did not have enough time to examine the cases in other than a most superficial way, they provided glowing references for their colleague, stressing that there was no argument whatever that his practice should be restricted. However, they did not include in this report *that they themselves had made him agree to a voluntary restriction.*

At the enquiry, counsel for one of the doctors asked a witness: 'The reason, and I want to be clear about this, the reason why he didn't insert the extraction of the undertaking in his report was that that would completely undermine Mr. Fitzpatrick's position in his dispute with the NEHB; is that not reasonable?'[25] The Committee was ambiguous about whether it was or not, since although it found all three doctors guilty of professional misconduct, the only sanction proposed for two of them was to be advised that in any future Report, they should also include any reservations they might have. The third doctor was to be 'admonished'.[26] In the event, the Council imposed no sanctions at all.

When Judge Harding Clark reported on the entire shocking business, she re-

---

[25] http://www.medicalcouncil.ie/_fileupload/news/Transcript_of_Inquiry_Day_2.pdf p. 4, line 23.
[26] http://www.medicalcouncil.ie/_fileupload/news/Findings_of_Fitness_to_Practise_Committee.pdf

corded her belief that the three doctors had acted 'out of compassion and collegiality.'[27] This, and their treatment by their licensing Council, sent a strong signal to
the public about the balance of the medical profession's 'compassion' as between
patients (in the abstract) and colleagues, and illustrates how cohesion can confuse
judgement. The three doctors claimed that by their secret agreement they had
done what was necessary to protect patients. Nevertheless, they lent their professional reputations to one side of a dispute where grievous suffering and even lives
were at stake, largely on the basis of 'trust' in a colleague.[28]

One of the charges against each Consultant was that he 'prepared the said
report under circumstances where he did not have adequate time or information,
or alternatively did not take adequate time or procure adequate information, properly to prepare the same.' Lay people may be surprised that although this was
'proved' against all three, in no case was it ruled to be professional misconduct.
This, coupled with the fact that the Medical Council did not impose even the
very light sanctions recommended by its Fitness to Practice Committee, will also
strengthen their belief that it is indeed high time for self-regulation by the Professions to come to an end.

As well as this, the case provides further evidence that whistleblowing should
be an essential component of whatever replaces self-regulation. Judge Harding
Clark recorded that 'If it were in the power of the Inquiry to make an award of
bravery to any person, it would be to the midwife who we shall call Ann who
made the first complaint to the North Eastern Health Board solicitor';[29] the Irish
Nurses Organisation produced a position paper on the need for it in the health
service; the head of the Health and Safety Authority has argued for action about
it; and the Minister has announced an intention to introduce it in some form. If it
is done properly in the Health Services, it would not be a huge step to extend it to
the whole bureaucracy.

Cohesion in the civil service

Returning to the civil service, the level of cohesion required for this to operate
is nothing like as high as that for the army or the garda. Civil servants are not
required to risk their lives in United Nations service nor in dealing with violent
criminals. Yet they do think of themselves as an in-group. The less their senior
people resist pressure from politicians to get them to undertake tasks which they

---

[27] http://www.dohc.ie/publications/pdf/lourdes.pdf?direct=1 p. 6.

[28] http://www.medicalcouncil.ie/_fileupload/news/Transcript_of_Inquiry_Day_4.pdf p. 17, line 24:
'once we had this preliminary discussion we looked at the cases. I would have to say that this was
based on a lot of mutual trust.'

[29] http://www.dohc.ie/publications/pdf/lourdes.pdf?direct=1 p. 188..

cannot do well and may not be able to do at all, the more publicity their resultant failures obtain. This adds to the pressure to turn inwards to look for the support of the group, which of course provides the environment for cover-ups. The more civil servants are aware that as a result the public outside sees them as being incompetent as well as overpaid, the more they tend to retreat into their own solidarity, and to think of where they work as a separate world, not completely subject to the laws of the State. What else could possibly explain the recent case uncovered by the Comptroller and Auditor-General, where an individual who stole several hundred euros from her Department was merely demoted and the theft was not reported to the police? Or where a County Manager felt justified in covering up theft by a councillor by imposing his own 'fine' of a donation to a charity?

The vestigial officer corps which might have been a constraint on actions like these if Brennan had got his way about the Administrative class, as discussed earlier, does not exist and cannot now be imposed. Consequently, formal arrangements for whistleblowing appear to be the only way of controlling inevitable civil service cover-ups due to collegiality. The best hope for these arrangements, as argued in Chapters VI and VII, would be that their very existence would prevent much wrongdoing, by increasing the fear of being found out.

For the Irish civil service to be a 'body of magistracy,' able to help constrain the growth of corporate faction, instead of being part of the problem as it is now, such a regime, allowing relief from the need to keep official secrets Act, is essential for it. The traditional system operated on the basis that the civil servant set out all the options for his Minister and then loyally acted according to the political decision. But Ministers were not then so determined on intervention, nor were they beholden to corporate funders to anything like the extent they are now. Both these pressures inevitably lead to politicisation of the civil service, and whistleblowing is at present the only safeguard against the harm which this causes. In the long run, it may be necessary to extend the crime of conspiracy to pervert the course of justice to include involvement in serious cover-ups.

Until public opinion reaches such a level of concern that it will insist on such a development, there are reasonably practicable interim measures which could be introduced with considerable benefit. Any appointments of civil servants to publicly-funded posts after retirement should be the exception rather than the rule, to try to make them less subservient to Ministers during their careers; and any that are made should be through a selection process which is really, and not just optically independent of politicians. The stringency of restrictions on civil servants taking up appointments in the private sector should increase with rank, and especially after retirement. And some realism should be brought to bear upon the gap between public and private sector pay.

Measuring pay differentials

Possibly because government Ministers' pay levels are linked to theirs, the upper ranks of the Irish civil service are among the highest paid bureaucrats in any EU country. This reflects highly effective rent-seeking in an economy which is only 1% of the EU total. The remarkable escalation in the remuneration of top civil servants in recent years has been brought about in two ways: firstly, the fiction they have been allowed to spread that civil servants can perform like private-sector managers, and consequently should be paid like them; and secondly because they have been able to call on tame private-sector rent-seekers to support their claim for 'comparability.' No worse example of this could be imagined than the 'benchmarking' process, which dared not speak the data on which recommendations for bringing the pay of higher civil servants 'into line' with that in private business were made.

This exercise can only have ignored the differences in terms of acceptance of responsibility and delivery of results. No one would grudge civil servants high financial rewards if they performed well, and in fact they are dealing with such large entities that even paying them more than now would be welcomed, if they did this. But what the public sees instead is high rewards for consistent failure to perform, indeed, the award of bonuses for *non-performance*. Wherever we have records, they confirm this, and the suspicion is widespread that even where we do not know what has gone on, the same pattern prevails.

The underlying causes of the widening gap between the earnings of civil servants and those who work in the so-called private sector are likely to increase it still further in the future. The evident future inability of even the largest rent-seeking firms in the economy, such as the banks, to pay 'final salary' pensions will be a powerful component in public awareness of this development. This is not in the long term interest of the civil service itself, because the wider this gap becomes, the more its members will come to resemble the apparatchiks of the Soviet Union, whose privileges were part of a 'pathology which deformed, and at the limit destroyed a political economy.'

One reason why the gap has been allowed to widen so much is that negotiators for the private side in national agreements have been poorly equipped with empirical data to support their own case. Research to provide this could be done in a similar manner to how useful estimates of the 'black economy' in the U.S.

have been made.[30] The result would be a crude enough measure, but it could at least show the order of magnitude of the premium currently obtainable for being able to avoid taking responsibility for failure.

Law or intervention – intellectual property

Chapter VIII put the case for beginning the attempt to replace intervention by law-making by installing an elite group in each Government department to develop specific legal alternatives to intervention which the mass of the civil service could be counted on to continue to favour. Nowhere has the country's loss from opting for intervention over legislation been so great as in relation to intellectual property, since this depends completely on laws.

Chapter I recounted how the Irish Free State joined the Paris Convention, the international Agreement which governs patents and trademarks, as a gesture of independence from Britain, in total ignorance of its implications. As the relevant Minister said when introducing the first Patents Act in 1927, 'the best thing for us to do is to legislate what the Convention requires.' The international intellectual property system has never operated in the interest of small countries, and in fact it has been a very effective agent of the interests of innovative multinational firms. The 1925 Hague Conference of the Paris Convention, for example, at which the Free State became a member, was also the one when it was agreed that the preservation of patent protection in any member country no longer required a firm to manufacture the related invention there. This of course was of enormous advantage to concentrated industries in advanced countries, which could now manufacture for the whole world in their plants in their home countries and so achieve economies of scale at home as well as patent protection abroad. If this provision of the Hague Conference had not come into effect, by introducing a patent system, the Free State might have been able to develop a number of small but innovative industries with a long-term future, instead of the dead-end of industrial development to which infant industry protection actually led it.

The contrast between Ireland and India is striking and instructive. When India became independent in 1947, it deliberately did not join the Paris Convention, which operates on the principle of reciprocity. This was because the Indians wanted to build up an indigenous pharmaceutical industry, and they understood that if they joined the Convention, they would have to give patent protection to the multinational pharmaceutical firms, and that this would prevent their own firms from getting started and growing. This policy was so successful that eventu-

---

[30] See, for example, McCrohan, Kevin F. and James D. Smith, 'A Consumer Expenditure Approach to Estimating the Size of the Underground Economy' Journal of Marketing 1986, 48-60.

ally the best of the new Indian firms wanted their country to join the Convention, because they had developed new drugs which had world-wide potential, and they wanted to be able to get patent protection for them in foreign markets.

While this was going on in India, independent Ireland persisted in operating intellectual property arrangements which serve the interests of firms in more advanced and bigger countries, notably, of course, the United States. So this country, too, has a pharmaceutical industry, but one which is owned and controlled elsewhere. Whereas India's industry is in the growing generic sector, that in Ireland is in the embattled patent-protected sector, which has already started to lose jobs.

Ireland's recent new copyright Act, as the relevant Minister of State at the time effectively admitted, was written to all intents and purposes by lobbyists for U.S. multinational interests. Once policies for attracting inward – especially American – foreign investment became dominant, it was inevitable that intellectual property laws would reflect this. It helps in attracting such investment to be able to say that the country's arrangements in this respect are what prospective investors are used to, and which have been devised to serve their interests. But if (when?) this policy fails, the Irish authorities will then have to think of turning to intellectual property legislation.

The TRIPs Agreement

Unfortunately, in very many ways it is already too late to gain from doing this. Since 1995, the options for countries to devise intellectual property laws to suit themselves have been greatly reduced. This is because of the Trade-related Intellectual Property section (TRIPs) annex to the Marrakesh agreement which set up the World Trade Organization (WTO). It is no exaggeration to describe this as a brutally self-interested initiative on the part of the United States to impose its own system on the world in the interest of its most advanced firms. This showed corporate 'faction' in operation at its worst, because it involved lobbying to extract American foreign commercial policy from the control of the State Department. Once freed from the constraints imposed by general foreign policy considerations, the U.S. Trade Representative became the focused and aggressive expression of American business interests. As the outstanding historian of TRIPs put it, 'in effect, 12 Corporations made public law for the world.'[31]

The EU, lobbied by its own largest firms, was willingly complicit in this, to the extent of scarcely bothering to keep its smaller member-countries in touch with the progress of the WTO negotiations. As well as this, Brussels policy is ob-

---

[31] Sell, Susan K., 2003: *Private Power, Public Law: The Globalization of Intellectual Property.* Cambridge, University Press, 93.

sessed by its ambition to have an EU-wide patent, like its successful Trade Mark and Design protection arrangements based in Alicante. Its argument is that this would reduce the cost of protecting inventions, ignoring the reality that the costs of litigation to protect grants are a large multiple of the cost of getting them. This is consequently a major deterrent to the use of patents by smaller firms (such as indigenously owned Irish firms mostly are).

Direct Protection of Innovation

For these reasons, it is now much more difficult than it was to develop the kinds of protection for investment in innovation that countries like Ireland need, within existing international arrangements. Whatever can still be done is likely to take the form of protecting innovation directly, rather than indirectly, as when intellectual property is used. As a senior English judge recently put it,

> One can, of course, postulate a different policy under which a monopoly might make sense. There are old or obvious ideas which take a lot of work, expense and time to develop and turn into something practical and successful. Without the incentive of a monopoly, people may not do that work or spend the time and money. The Fosamax case, Teva v Gentili, is an example of an obvious invention which cost lots to bring to market. But patent law provided no protection for all that investment because the basic invention was obvious.[32]

Chapter IX, 'A Patent System to Suit Ireland', emerged from an EU-commissioned study on the 'direct protection' approach.[33] Since that appeared, two developments have put it into practical effect. The first of these is the European Database Directive, which gives protection to compilations which cannot claim the level of originality required for copyright or for a patent. Even more promising is U.S 'Orphan' Drug protection, to encourage the development of new drugs for diseases suffered by relatively few patients. This has been remarkably successful, resulting in 12 times more drugs of the type needed, with measurable declines in relevant death rates.

This is a system of protection of innovation, not invention. Protection is granted, not for the concept of the new drug, nor even for laboratory proofs that it is effective, but only for the fully developed and tested drug, ready to go onto the market. It is this that is protected directly. There is no reason why the same principle could not be applied far more widely. If such remarkable results as those for Orphan drugs can be achieved in an area where patents work best (because their present form, laid down by the 1952 U.S. Act and its copies in other coun-

---

[32] From: Angiotech Pharm., Inc. v. Conor MedSystems Inc., [2007] EWCA Civ 5, 50 (Court of Appeal 2007) (Jacob, L.J.) , aff'g, [2006] EWHC 260 (Pat) (Pumfrey, J.)(High Court 2006).

[33] See Chapter IX above.

tries, was specifically designed to protect pharmaceutical inventions) how much greater must the untapped potential be in areas where patents work badly or not at all? It could be put into effect outside the restrictive TRIPs framework, through co-operation between countries with similar interests. The Danes, for example, have been especially active in trying to get a better regime for smaller, indigenous firms, through patent litigation insurance.[34]

No Irish support for better laws

It is unlikely that Ireland will figure to any significant extent in such efforts. Forfas and Enterprise Ireland were recently offered the opportunity to match funds already awarded by the European Patent Office for research on applying the Orphan Drug principle to the inventions of smaller firms. The amount was trivial by their standards and their money would have added little to the value of the research itself. But it would have put them into a position of leadership amongst the other EU states in initiating a change, if the research showed that this was warranted. Their rejection of this idea is altogether understandable in the light of their preference for intervention rather than better laws.

Obtaining improvements through legal changes holds no attraction for members of rent-seeking bodies, such as those charged with administering industrial policy. Devising better laws does not lead to bigger budgets and more staff for these, whereas distributing grants and organizing other so-called 'incentives' does. Chapter X, 'The Financing of New Businesses,' was originally a paper which aroused no interest from the Irish authorities, but from which the Business Start-up and Expansion schemes emerged in Britain after it had been published by the Cabinet Office there.[35] As mentioned in Chapter I, the Industrial Development Authority later resisted a political initiative to have the second of these initiatives copied here, precisely because providing new or better law – no matter how effective it might be in achieving an objective – would take power out of their hands.

Whether because of this foot-dragging or not, the Irish law in this case has not been well drafted. The original intention of tax relief on equity investment was to provide a source of seed capital, because this is something that only the State can do on any considerable scale. However, in practice this relief it has been predominantly obtained by businesses in low-risk fields which should find it possible to obtain finance from venture capital firms if not indeed ordinary banking finance. This distortion of the original objective caused the abandonment of the Business

---

[34] See Kingston W., 2007: 'Better Patents for Smaller Firms: Insurance, Incontestability, Arbitration?' Intellectual Property Quarterly 1-18.

[35] It formed a major part of Industrial Innovation 1987: London, the Stationery Office.

Expansion Scheme in Britain, whereas lobbying in Ireland has actually brought about an extension to its range.

The mirage of research funding

The currently fashionable policy in this area is based on the belief that money spent on scientific research in Ireland will eventually end up in employment and profits here. This exists in a particularly naïve form amongst politicians, as Ministers' personal espousal of the spectacular failure of Media Lab Europe illustrates. In this, yet once more, the inability of the civil service to act as a counterbalancing 'magistracy' is apparent.[36] The result of Ministers being sold on this particular belief has been a very great increase in the amount of funds allocated to research, mainly through Science Foundation Ireland (SFI). Unfortunately, the belief is unsound in two ways: Firstly, its linear view that science leads to innovation and then to products on the market only operates in a limited number of fields. In others, much innovation takes place on the basis of little science or before the science which explains it has been done. Secondly, there is no point in producing new ideas and information, except to the extent that there are entrepreneurs available who can grasp their meaning and are ready to take the risks of exploiting them in the country.

The second point can be illustrated immediately. When the Marine Institute was established, one of its competitive research awards was won by a proposal to investigate the potential of rock engineering in cliffs as a means of capturing ocean wave energy. This was done by a multi-disciplinary team from Ireland, Sweden and the U.S., and their Report was published by the Institute.[37] It was not taken up by Irish entrepreneurs and investors, but instead has now begun to be exploited in the Faroe Islands. It can reasonably be expected, therefore, that when the new technology eventually comes to be applied to the vast energy resource on the West coast, it will be through equipment from foreign, not Irish industry, as is already the case with Irish exploitation of wind power. As stressed in earlier Chapters, a rent-seeking economy such as Ireland predominantly is, conditions its investors to easy pickings, and certainly does not tend to produce entrepreneurs who are interested in or capable of taking up the results of research and turning them into saleable products. But without investors of this kind, any valuable information which comes out of public funding of research will more than likely be exploited abroad.

---

[36] See http://www.audgen.gov.ie/documents/annualreports/2004/Vol1Eng.pdf

[37] Infrastructure and R & D Projects supported under Measure 8 (Marine Research Measure) compiled by Elizabeth Hyland, November 2000

Protecting research results

An aspect of increased public expenditure on research is encouragement of recipients of awards, mainly universities, to seek patent protection for their results. Again, this is based upon limited understanding of the value which a relatively small number of Universities in the United States have obtained from 1991 legislation which allows them to hold patents on the results of research carried out with public funds. But this encouragement, which includes funding for University patenting from Enterprise Ireland, ignores the reality that any form of intellectual property has to be protected in the Courts by its owner, and the cost of the litigation to do this can be prohibitive, especially in the United States.

In a 2001 study for the EU, for example, it was found that every patent owned in the U.S. by small European firms that had any value, was infringed there.[38] It is next to impossible for such firms to assert their rights successfully, because of the biased litigation system and the readiness of U.S. infringers to intimidate smaller firms with the threat of imposing litigation costs on them which they will be unable to stand. This applies to copyrights, designs, and new plant varieties, as well as to patents. Neither could any Irish University risk the cost of litigation in the U.S. Even if there was no shortage of entrepreneurs, these obstacles would virtually ensure that anything valuable which comes out of SFI funding will be exploited abroad. The results of Media Lab Europe's patenting activity should dampen excessive political hopes in this area: the fire sale of their patent applications which had cost around €0.75 million, realized only €40,000. However, the results of SFI funding can hardly be anything like as bad as this, and a practical suggestion which could help to improve them significantly is outlined below.

'Contingency fee' litigation

Firms in the U.S. have a particular advantage over those in any other country in terms of protecting their intellectual property, whether this has come about through their own research, or by licensing, as is likely to be the case with any SFI-funded inventions. This is that in the U.S., 'contingency fee' arrangements with lawyers are legal, which they are not on this side of the Atlantic. These are quite different from what is known here as 'no foal, no fee', in which a lawyer takes a case on the condition that his fees will only be paid if he wins it with costs awarded, meaning that they are payable by the opposing side.

In the U.S., each side pays its own costs, win or lose. On a contingency fee basis, the client does not have any liability to pay his own lawyers, but if he wins,

[38] EU Report, Enforcing Small Firms' Patent Rights, 2001 Available at http://www.cordis.lu/innovationpolicy/studies/2001/management03.htm

these lawyers are then entitled to receive a large share of whatever damages are awarded. 40 per cent is typical for this and a 50-50 split is not uncommon, especially if there is an appeal. Some competent legal practices specialise in this kind of work. As well as this, U.S. courts can and do award triple damages for deliberate infringement. As a result of such provisions, a patentee with a good case has a much better chance of defending it in U.S. courts than anywhere else.

However, a serious drawback remains. Although in contingency fee cases the U.S. legal firm is investing the expertise of its staff at its own risk, and the prospect of a very large payoff is a valuable motivating factor for them, its client still has to pay all related costs, such as for discovery of documents, expert witnesses, Court charges and the like. Infringers are very skilful at pushing such charges up, as a way of intimidating opponents. In one case where the figures are available, the UK owner of a U.S. patent has had to finance costs getting close to $0.25m., on his way to the appeal Court. Levels of cost like this are enough to put off indigenous Irish firms, as well as Universities, even if they are able to find a law firm to take their case on a contingency fee basis.

An Irish opportunity

Since all the earlier Chapters were written on the premise that one should not complain without offering some suggestion for improvement, it is appropriate that this updating of them should end in the same way. It does so by calling attention to an opportunity the U.S. contingency fee arrangements offer to the Irish industrial development authorities. This has all the characteristics which would enable it to be administered by a bureaucracy, the most important of which, of course, is ability to escape from individual blame for failure.

They could set up a programme to fund only the incidental costs of U.S. litigation where an Irish-based firm or University is involved and has found a law firm in that country to take its case on a contingency fee basis. The 'cover' they need for their decisions would be provided for them by the agreement of a U.S. legal firm to take the case. Irish bureaucrats would not have to do any evaluation of projects or of a firm's chances of winning a case, because they could be sure that no law firm will take a case on a contingency payment basis unless it considers that it has a good chance of making money out of it. Although the amounts of these incidental costs are considerable, they are small compared with the costs of the lawyers, and they would all be Court-related and so easy to audit. The 'cover' of those administering the scheme could even be enhanced by having an approved list of contingency fee lawyers, and just as support is provided for University patenting at present, the cost to firms of negotiating contingency fee support from one of these firms could also be subsidized.

As the threat to manufacturing jobs in Ireland escalates, the industrial promotion agencies are looking for ways of making location here attractive to service industries. A programme such as that proposed could tempt businesses which depend upon intellectual property, even from the U.S. itself, since unless this property can be protected it is worthless. It is particularly relevant to protecting the results of SFI funding. By definition, this should only be provided to projects which have a global potential, meaning that patent protection in the United States would be essential for them.

Such an initiative should also be a powerful boost to current efforts to get more research and development (R&D) activity to Ireland. It could counterbalance the recent EU ruling that tax exemption on patent royalties will also have to apply in respect of inventions made elsewhere in the Union. And it would greatly improve the potential for joint research projects between Irish and U.S. Universities, because the litigation support would presumably apply to anything that came out of their mutual efforts - and the U.S. University could not get it at home.

The very existence of such a scheme would in fact be a powerful deterrent to intimidation by infringers in that country, so that the number of cases where it would actually be necessary to put up cash would likely be few. This is because virtually all decisions to intimidate are taken by middle management in large firms. In terms of effect on the career path of someone at this level, it is one thing to bully a smaller firm or University if it can be assumed that they do not have the resources to resist. It is an entirely different thing if there is potential backing from a government-funded body. In that case, the prudent course for such a manager is to recommend that his firm negotiates for the intellectual property it wants to use, instead of infringing it.

Conclusion

The evidence and arguments in the earlier chapters on the harm of credulity in the value of State action, might be taken as reflecting bias against the public service. In fact, the opposite is the case. This questioning of Irish policies is based upon the conviction of the need for a 'body of magistracy' to check and restrain corporate interests, above all in the context of a multi-seat proportional representation electoral system.

There is no evident candidate for this vital balancing role apart from the civil service, which is why the key chapter in this collection is that on 'A New Agenda for Public Sector Reform.' The modest proposal which this makes for replacing intervention by creative lawmaking, could be the start of a useful reduction in opportunities for rent-seeking. The addition of whistleblowing throughout the public service could then transform its efficiency as well as its morale, as intervention is reduced.

It may be recalled that one of the objectors to the latter proposal claimed that 'the civil service is full of good people, who only want to do their best for the country.' But individuals can only do their best – or even do any good at all – if the institution in which they work is itself healthy.

In the Irish context, then, it will take at least a couple of institutional changes to set their energies free, and by doing so, to promote a wider release of the public's creativity in its own interest.

Acknowledgements

Ten of the foregoing Chapters originally appeared in the following publications, and I would like to acknowledge my debt to their Editors, whose suggestions improved my original submissions to them in every case.

'Belief in the superior wisdom of the State...' In *Ideas at Work: Essays in Honour of Geoffrey MacKechnie*, Frank Litton, Tony Farmar, Frank Scott-Lennon (eds.) Dublin, A & A Farmar 2006,161 – 176.

'The Lemmings of Democracy' *Studies* Winter 1976

'Why Ireland failed to keep up' *Studies,* 1994, 252-64

'Entrepreneurship or Rent-Seeking?' In Andrew E. Burke (ed.) *Enterprise and the Irish Economy* (1995). Dublin, Oak Tree Press, 249-67.

'Innovation: New Property Rights are Better than State Involvement' In, *Competition and Industry: The Irish Experience*, D. McAleese (ed.) 1989. Dublin, Gill and Macmillan, 71-78.

'What Can We Do About the Civil Service?' *Studies*, 90, 2001, 320-330

'Systemic Corporate Failure of Public Administration:' Reflections on the Travers Report' S*tudies*, 94, (376), 2005, 385 - 395

'An Alternative Agenda for Public Service Reform' *Administration*, 52, (1), 2004, 35 - 45

'A Patent System To Suit Ireland?' Irish Banking Review, Autumn 1987, 21-29.

'The Financing of New Businesses' In *Industrial Innovation* 1979: London, HMSO for the Cabinet Office, 37-43.

Index

A

academic thinking 34, 53, 60, 62, 102
accountancy, growth of 65
administrative evil 94
Aer Lingus 35, 84
Africa 15
  fate of democratic regimes in 15, 49
Airship R101 69
Allied Irish Banks 84
apparatchiks
  destructive effect of privileges of 130
Appeals Commissioners
  (Revenue) 124
arbitration
  for patentees 101–102
  for US Federal employees 37
Arklow
  siting of fertilizer factory 8
Attorney-General 80
Australia
  and patent system 97

B

Baring's Bank 73
  City of London investigation of 85
Beddy, Dr J. P. 7
beneficial ownership 91
Bismarck 42, 94
black economy in the U.S. 130
'body of magistracy' 121, 129, 138
Boeing
  and public travel by jet 103
  Hydrofoil 110
bourgeoisie
  in Marx 15, 94, 115
  in Schumpeter 18
Brendan Smith case 123
Brennan, Joseph 118, 129
bribery 117, 119
British Biotech 73
British civil service
  and Sir Warren Fisher 119
  helping Irish Free State 8
British Labour Party 17
Brussels
  and IP rights 39, 132

and lobbying by US interests 10–11, 115
  transfers from 34, 41, 55
Bruton, John 12
bureaucracy
  and avoidance of blame 122, 125, 137
  and whistleblowing 75, 128
  growth of 46
  limiting innovation 32
  limits to 36, 121
  moderating influence 20
  modern v. old 73
  pathologies of 73, 74, 85, 86, 87, 120
  politicised 118
  Prussian imperial 95
  role of 2, 37, 72, 94
bureaucrat-speak 82
Business Start-up and Expansion Schemes 12,
  134
Butler, Lord 119

C

Cabinet collective responsibility 7
Cadet School (Army) 125
Carnegie, Andrew 5
Carroll's (tobacco firm) 4
Central Bank building 89
Central Statistics Office 6
Challenger disaster 95
Churchill, Winston S. 86
civil servants
  and 1925 Hague Conference 9
  and interventionist policies 46
  and private sector pay 130
  as managers 51, 119, 121
  as suppliers of national statistics 59
  avoidance of attributable failure 73, 83, 122,
  123
  conflict of duty v. career 70, 95
  education and social class 20, 24, 68, 83
  group solidarity 128
  growing complexity of tasks 123
  independence of higher 74, 94
  interventionist policies 36
  limits to capacity 121
  Ministers, subservience to 22, 81, 83, 120,
  121
  morale 77